YORK NOTES

General Editors: Professor A.N. Jeffares (*University of Stirling*) & Professor Suheil Bushrui (*American University of Beirut*)

William Shakespeare

A MIDSUMMER NIGHT'S DREAM

Notes by R.P. Draper

BA PHD (NOTTINGHAM)
Professor of English, University of Aberdeen

LONGMAN
YORK PRESS

YORK PRESS
Immeuble Esseily, Place Riad Solh, Beirut.

LONGMAN GROUP UK LIMITED
Longman House, Burnt Mill, Harlow,
Essex CM20 2JE, England
Associated companies, branches and representatives
throughout the world

First published 1980
Sixth impression 1989

ISBN 0-582-02285-1

Produced by Longman Group (FE) Ltd.
Printed in Hong Kong

Contents

Part 1

Introduction

ENGLAND IN THE LATTER HALF of the sixteenth century was a small country ruled over by a virgin Queen, Elizabeth I, whose main aim was to save her country from the dissension with which it had been plagued for a hundred and more years before her reign. The memory of the Wars of the Roses, in which claimants from the rival families of York and of Lancaster struggled to gain and hold the throne of England, still lingered in people's minds, and Shakespeare was to write at length in his history plays, covering the period from the deposition of Richard II (1367–1400), to the reign of Elizabeth's father, Henry VIII (who lived from 1491 to 1547), on the dangers of disorder and civil war. England under Henry had become a Protestant country, with the monarch instead of the Pope as head of the Church, but many still held to the Catholic faith, and the fear of Catholic rebellion was still strong. The greatest event of Shakespeare's early manhood was the defeat in 1588 of the huge Armada which the Catholic Philip of Spain had despatched, with the blessing of the Pope, to conquer England and win it back for what he regarded as the true religion.

With this victory the country gained confidence in itself, but the cautious government still insisted on the need for obedience to the monarch and respect for the established order of society. Men were encouraged to look up to the Queen as an exalted figure embodying the ideals of chastity, justice and wisdom. Edmund Spenser, the greatest Elizabethan poet before Shakespeare, wrote in his *Shepherd's Calendar* (1579):

> *Of fair Elisa be your silver song,*
> *That blessed wight,*
> *The flower of virgins: may she flourish long*
> *In princely plight!*

And Shakespeare's 'fair vestal, throned by the west' (*A Midsummer Night's Dream*, II.1.158) is another of the countless tributes that were paid to Elizabeth in the literature of the time. While, with shrewd political calculation, she steered the country on a safe moderate course, the Queen surrounded herself with courtiers. They praised her extravagantly, dressed brilliantly, as she did herself, and, though often intriguing for her hand in marriage, and the power which that would bring, kept up a pretence that the days of medieval chivalry, with its code of bravery and honour, were still alive.

Society was, however, changing. Men might be taught to know their place and keep within it, but the new economic conditions favoured mobility. The medieval pattern of trade and manufacture conducted by 'guilds', which laid down conditions and restricted entry to various businesses and professions, was giving way to the greater energy, and sometimes ruthlessness, of boldly enterprising individuals. The discovery of the New World changed men's geographical horizons, and though its riches were first exploited by the Spaniards, enmity between England and Spain gave excuse for men such as Drake and Raleigh to carve a share for themselves as well, either by thinly disguised piracy of Spanish ships, or by colonisation of parts of America to which the Spaniards had not yet penetrated. Trade was extended eastwards as well, and Richard Hakluyt, in his *Principal Navigations, Voyages and Discoveries of the English Nation* (1589), was able to ask: 'Which of the kings of this land before her Majesty, had their banners ever seen in the Caspian Sea? Which of them hath ever dealt with the Emperor of Persia?' The intellectual discoveries of Galileo and Copernicus, which were to revolutionise men's conception of the universe in which they lived, were as yet reaching only a few of the more intelligent and enquiring minds in Elizabethan England. The majority continued to think of the earth as fixed and stable, the centre of all things, round which the sun, moon, planets and stars moved in divinely ordained orbits. In other matters of learning, however, developments were taking place which were beginning to have more extensive effect. The universities had brought new scholarship to the study of the classical languages of Greece and Rome, new ideas were developing in medicine, mathematics and science, and the traditional view that man should concern himself only with knowledge that would help him to find his spiritual way to the next world was giving way, if only gradually, to knowledge that would enhance his understanding and enjoyment of life in this world.

Perhaps most important of all, the very nature of the English language was changing. Its grammar was being simplified and its vocabulary enormously increased by a flood of borrowings from foreign languages, especially Latin and Greek. A few purists objected, but the tide was irresistible. Writers soon gained confidence in the enhanced resources of the language and began to produce works which could challenge comparison with the best, both of the classical past, and of more recent achievements in Italy and France. For instance Sir Philip Sidney produced the elaborately decorative *Arcadia* (c.1580), and the sequence of love-sonnets, *Astrophel and Stella* (some time prior to 1586). Edmund Spenser paid compliment to Queen Elizabeth when he wrote his long and complex poem, *The Faerie Queene,* the first three books of which appeared in 1590 and the rest in 1596. Both of these poets wrote, however, exclusively for courtly and aristocratic readers. The popular art-form, which also appealed to all classes of society, was the drama. Through writers like Lyly, Peele, Greene, Kyd and Marlowe this developed from the crude, ranting melodrama and knock-about farce of the mid-century interludes and plays into a subtle and expressive medium which could be used by Shakespeare to realise the possibilities of the flourishing English language to the full.

Shakespeare's life

William Shakespeare was born at Stratford-upon-Avon in 1564. Tradition has it that the precise date of his birth was St George's Day, 23 April, but this may have arisen by confusion with the day of his death. The only exact record is that of his christening, 26 April 1564. His father, John Shakespeare, was a businessman in Stratford, and prominent in local affairs until the late 1570s when, it seems, he fell into debt. His mother, Mary Arden, came from a higher social background, being the daughter of a gentleman and landowner, Robert· Arden.

Little is known of Shakespeare's early life. He probably attended the Stratford School, where he would have received a good grounding in Latin, and he may later have become a schoolmaster for a while. Stories about his having been apprenticed to a butcher (John Aubrey says that 'when he kill'd a calfe, he would doe it in a high style, and make a speech') and having stolen deer from the park of Sir Thomas Lucy of Charlecote, near Stratford, are without solid foundation. In November 1582 he married Anne Hathaway, of Shottery, a woman eight years older than himself, and their first daughter, Susanna, was christened on 26 May 1583. The dates suggest that Anne may have already been pregnant by him before they married, but since a contract may have been made prior to the church wedding, which in Elizabethan times would have been regarded as tantamount to marriage, there is no need to suppose, as some have done, that Shakespeare was reluctantly compelled to marry to save his child from the brand of bastardy. Two other children were born to Anne in 1585, the twins Hamnet and Judith, who were christened on 2 February. Both of the girls were later married to Stratford men, Susanna to John Hall, 5 June 1607, and Judith to Thomas Quiney, 10 February 1616; but the boy, Hamnet, only lived till he was 11– his burial took place at Stratford on 11 August 1596.

For whatever reason – because he wanted to make his fortune, or because he had already been attracted to the profession of acting, or because he was compelled to leave Stratford under a cloud – some time in the late 1580s Shakespeare made his way, without his family, to London and became an actor-dramatist. He first joined the group of actors who enjoyed the protection of Lord Pembroke, and so were known as Lord Pembroke's Men, or Company, but later became a member of the Lord Chamberlain's Men, who, on the accession of James I to the throne of England, were honoured with the title of the King's Men. To begin with he was both actor and writer, his earliest plays being the three parts of *Henry VI*, *Richard III*, the tragedy of *Titus Andronicus* and the comedies, *The Comedy of Errors*, *The Taming of the Shrew* and *The Two Gentlemen of Verona*. All of these were probably written by 1592, the year in which Robert Greene, one of the group of university-educated dramatists whose plays were popular when Shakespeare arrived in London, wrote maliciously on his death-bed, urging his friends not to trust the players any longer, 'for there is an upstart Crow, beautified with our feathers, that with his *Tygers hart wrapt in a Players hyde,* supposes he is as well able to bombast out a blank verse as the best of you: and being an absolute *Iohannes fac totum* [Johnny-do-all], is in his owne conceit the onely Shake-scene in a countrey' *(Greenes Groats-worth of Wit).* This is clearly a jealous reference to Shakespeare (it parodies the line from Part 3 of *Henry VI*, I.4.137, in which York addresses the fierce virago, Queen Margaret, as 'O tiger's heart wrapp'd in a woman's hide'), and suggests that he had already, by 1592, established himself as one of the leading men in the theatre of his day.

Tradition has it that among Shakespeare's roles as an actor were Adam in *As You Like It* (1599) and the ghost in *Hamlet* (1600–1). These are minor parts, and though he may have taken more important roles (one of his contemporaries says that he was an excellent actor), he became so busy as a playwright that most of his time must have been occupied in composition. In the 1590s he wrote seven more comedies besides those already mentioned, culminating in *Twelfth Night* (1599–1600), four more history plays, two more tragedies and two narrative poems, *Venus and Adonis* and *The Rape of Lucrece*, as well as the bulk of the Sonnets which were published in 1609. At the beginning of the new century tragedy began to occupy him almost completely, and he wrote a series of plays which are the most passionate and profound that England has ever known: *Hamlet*, *Othello* (1604–5), *Macbeth* (1605–6), *King Lear* (1605–6) and *Antony and Cleopatra* (1606–7).

During the whole of this period Shakespeare lived and worked in London, occupying lodgings not far from the theatres on which his life was centred; but he did not forget Stratford. The right to a coat of arms, the sign of a man's status as a gentleman, which his father tried to establish for his family, but had to abandon, was taken up again and secured by Shakespeare in 1596. In the following year he bought a substantial house in Stratford called New Place, and he acquired other property in 1602. From time to time he made return visits to his native town, and from about 1610 he made it his home once more. Shakespeare continued, however, to write plays and to visit London. The so-called 'last plays' (*Pericles, Cymbeline, The Winter's Tale* and *The Tempest*) belong to the years from 1608–12, and – though it is dangerous to try to infer Shakespeare's state of mind from interpretation of his work – indicate a certain mellowing of outlook and a preoccupation with the relations between parents and children which seem to suggest a man who is beginning to take stock of the past and think of the future in terms of the handing on of life to the next generation. His final play was *Henry VIII,* written in collaboration with John Fletcher, 1613. This was also the year in which the Globe Theatre was destroyed by fire.

Early in January 1616 Shakespeare made his will. Bequests were made to Stratford acquaintances and to his actor-friends, Burbage, Heminges and Condell (the latter pair became, after his death, the editors of the first complete edition of Shakespeare's works, the First Folio of 1623); but the major part of his estate was made over to his family. He died on 23 April 1616.

Date of *A Midsummer Night's Dream*

A Midsummer Night's Dream is one of the earlier comedies of Shakespeare. It is impossible to date it precisely. We know that it was written by 1598 as it is mentioned by Francis Meres in his *Palladis Tamia* of that date, along with other comedies, tragedies and histories by Shakespeare. Some commentators, influenced by the importance of Theseus's marriage to Hippolyta and by the entry of the fairies at the end of Act V to bless the marriage-bed, think that it may have been written for a wedding. The performance of a play was a usual form of entertainment on such occasions in Shakespeare's time, and various weddings in the 1590s have been suggested as likely occasions. However, the evidence is far from conclusive. Because of Titania's speech in II.1.81–117, describing winds and floods in the countryside, which they take as a topical reference to bad summer weather in the year when the play was written, some commentators have also sought for records of a particularly bad year in the 1590s which would pinpoint the date of the play. However, even if such an argument were to be accepted, there is no general agreement on which year could be regarded as an especially bad one. The most that can be said is that the play was probably written between 1593 and 1596, with 1594 as a reasonable guess. This would place it after *The Comedy of Errors, Two Gentlemen of Verona* and *Love's Labour's Lost* and before *Much Ado About Nothing, As You Like It* and *Twelfth Night.*

Sources

Like those comedies which come before and after it *A Midsummer Night's Dream* is inspired by the romantic stories which were popular in the Middle Ages and continued to be so in Elizabethan times – tales of ideal love and marvellous adventures which carry the reader away into a world of richly coloured fantasy remote from the comparatively tawdry business of everyday life. Unlike most of Shakespeare's plays, however, it does not have a readily identifiable source, and it appears to be one of the rare examples of Shakespeare inventing his own plot. He may have taken a hint from Chaucer's *Knight's Tale*, itself a highly romantic story, which begins with a reference to the conquests of Theseus (as in Shakespeare, given the unclassical title of 'duke'), and, in particular, to his defeat of 'Ipolita', queen of the female warriors known as 'Amazons', and his subsequent marriage to her. The same Theseus material, with the addition of references to his many other love exploits, can also be found in Plutarch's *Lives of the Noble Grecians and Romans*, which Shakespeare certainly knew in Sir Thomas North's translation of 1579, as he used it extensively in later plays such as *Antony and Cleopatra* and *Coriolanus*. Ovid's *Metamorphoses,* another book which Shakespeare knew well, is probably the source for the story of the play-within-the-play, 'Pyramus and Thisby', and, as Stanley Wells says, the ridiculously wooden verse of Golding's translation of the *Metamorphoses* may have prompted him to a burlesque version of it. Some details for the fairies may likewise have been taken from Ovid, and from an old romance called *Huon of Bordeaux,* a dramatic version of which was performed at the end of 1593; and Reginald Scot's *The Discoverie of Witchcraft* (1584) may have contributed something both to the fairies and Bottom's transformation by means of the ass's head. But to none of these is Shakespeare's debt great, and the fact remains that the substance of the plot, together with the inter-weaving of the various strands into one whole, are original.

If there is a major source for *A Midsummer Night's Dream* it should be sought for in the folk-tales and superstitions which were kept alive by oral tradition rather than books. Elizabethan England was still, notwithstanding the growing importance and size of London, a rural society which believed, or at least half-believed, in witches, ghosts, hobgoblins and supernatural beings, both good and evil. It is to this order of creatures that Shakespeare's fairies belong, especially the mischievous Puck, Robin Goodfellow, whose very English nature is described within the play itself (at II.1.32–57). Oberon and Titania are more imposing creatures, with something of the aura of classical and oriental deities about them, but they, too, despite their Indian affinities, belong essentially to the English countryside. Their 'source' is in the culture which Shakespeare imbibed from his Stratford-upon-Avon boyhood, and with which even the London audiences of his manhood were still familiar.

The Elizabethan theatre

The circumstances in which *A Midsummer Night's Dream* was originally seen by Elizabethan audiences were very different from those in which it is to be seen in present-day theatres. The Elizabethan stage was essentially a raised platform, some 28ft long, and from 24 to 43ft wide, protruding into an open yard surrounded by wooden galleries. Trap-doors were let into the floor of the stage, through which devils, fairies and other supernatural beings could make their exits and entrances, if so needed; or if deities were required to descend from Heaven, they could be let down in a 'throne' from another trap-door in the short roof which covered the platform. At the back of the main stage was a smaller recess, or inner-stage, known as the 'study', which could be curtained off from the view of the audience. This might be used to represent places like Titania's 'bower', or Prospero's cell in *The Tempest*, or Juliet's tomb in *Romeo and Juliet*. Above it would be a balcony (the 'chamber'), suitable for the scene in *Romeo and Juliet* where Juliet enters 'above at a window' and speaks to Romeo below in the 'orchard' (II.2). Above this again would be the 'music gallery' where the music, which was an important part of much Elizabethan drama, and which is especially important in Shakespeare's comedies, would be played.

The Elizabethan theatre derived its basic shape from the old English inns, built round an enclosed courtyard, in which performances most frequently took place until London's new public theatres were built, and which even then continued to be the usual places of performances in country towns. The first of the new theatres, the name of which was 'The Theatre', was built in 1576 on the south bank of the Thames by James Burbage, father of Richard Burbage, who was to become the first great Shakespearean actor. It was soon followed by other theatres, such as the Curtain, Hope, Rose, Fortune and Globe. Among these the Fortune was square-shaped, the Globe octagonal, or, in a general sense, round (hence the reference in the Prologue of Shakespeare's history play, *Henry V*, to 'this wooden O'). Built in part from the materials of the dismantled Theatre, and opened in 1599, the Globe was to become the most famous of all Elizabethan theatres as the home of the Lord Chamberlain's Men, the company of players which Shakespeare himself joined in 1594, and hence the major site for the production of all his plays from 1599 onwards.

All these theatres were open to the sky. Only the galleries, where the better-off spectators sat, and the stage itself, were roofed. Ordinary playgoers – workmen and their wives, apprentices and their sweethearts, country-folk who had come in from the nearby villages – stood for a penny each in the uncovered yard surrounding the stage

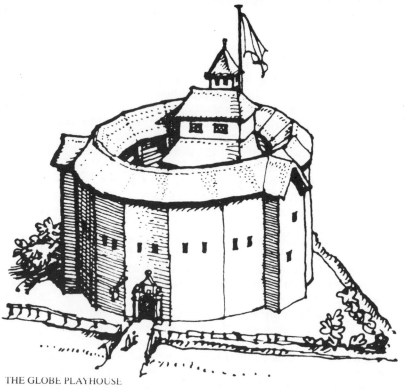

THE GLOBE PLAYHOUSE

The theatre, originally built by James Burbage in 1576, was made of wood (Burbage had been trained as a carpenter). It was situated to the north of the River Thames on Shoreditch in Finsbury Fields. There was trouble with the lease of the land, and so the theatre was dismantled in 1598, and reconstructed 'in an other forme' on the south side of the Thames as the Globe. Its sign is thought to have been a figure of the Greek hero Hercules carrying the globe. It was built in six months, its galleries being roofed with thatch. This caught fire in 1613 when some smouldering wadding, from a cannon used in a performance of Shakespeare's *Henry VIII*, lodged in it. The theatre was burnt down, and when it was rebuilt again on the old foundations, the galleries were roofed with tiles.

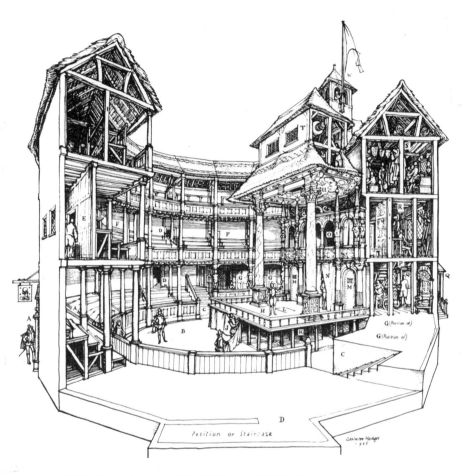

A CONJECTURAL RECONSTRUCTION OF THE INTERIOR OF
THE GLOBE PLAYHOUSE

AA Main entrance
 B The Yard
CC Entrances to lowest gallery
 D Entrance to staircase and upper galleries
 E Corridor serving the different sections of the middle gallery
 F Middle gallery ('Twopenny Rooms')
 G 'Gentlemen's Rooms or Lords Rooms'
 H The stage
 J The hanging being put up round the stage
 K The 'Hell' under the stage
 L The stage trap, leading down to the Hell
MM Stage doors

N Curtained 'place behind the stage'
O Gallery above the stage, used as required sometimes by musicians, sometimes by spectators, and often as part of the play
P Back-stage area (the tiring-house)
Q Tiring-house door
R Dressing-rooms
S Wardrobe and storage
T The hut housing the machine for lowering enthroned gods, etc., to the stage
U The 'Heavens'
W Hoisting the playhouse flag

and took their chance with the weather. Noblemen who wished to see the play were accommodated, at a higher price, in those parts of the galleries which were nearest the stage, but partitioned off from the rest of the theatre, while the 'gallants' (young men who prided themselves on their wit and fashion) paid for the privilege of sitting on the stage, as conspicuous to the whole audience as the actors themselves.

Certain indoor theatres were built in the early seventeenth century, and even in the sixteenth century the boy-actors from St Paul's gave indoor performances, but it was for the open-air theatres that Shakespeare wrote most of his work, and it was these which shaped his ideas of dramatic art. There, performances took place in the afternoon by natural daylight. The artificial illumination, and consequently elaborate lighting effects, of the modern theatre were unavailable, and there was little scope for the elaborate scene-setting which is made possible in the modern theatre by the combination of lighting and sophisticated stage machinery and by ending the stage at the line of the footlights instead of allowing it to protrude into the middle of the audience. Some simple stage properties were used, such as the 'bank' on which Titania sleeps (II.1.249–53) and the ass's head which is put on Bottom's shoulders (perhaps while he is out of the audience's sight behind the 'bank'), but most scenic effects were created by words, time and place were communicated mainly by words, and a character like Oberon would even make himself 'invisible' in words (II.1.186). The willingness of audiences to let their imaginations be acted upon by the poetic resources of language, instead of insisting on realistic illusions, was a major feature of Elizabethan dramatic practice. What might have seemed a disadvantage was turned into a great asset, for the minds of the audience went wherever the actors' words directed them. Scenes did not have to be changed; one set of actors left the stage and another set came on immediately after them, indicating, if necessary, through their speeches where they were and what they were doing. The result was great speed and fluidity of action, making it quite credible, as Shakespeare claims in the Prologue to *Romeo and Juliet,* that the performance of a play would be but 'the two hours' traffic of our stage'.

The relationship between actor and audience must also have been more intimate than in a modern theatre (except where this is deliberately provided for by an experiment like the twentieth-century 'theatre in the round', which uses a centrally placed stage surrounded by the audience on all sides). By advancing to the forward part of the stage the actor could speak an 'aside' to the audience as if taking them into his confidence, and deliver a soliloquy – a speech in which a character alone on the stage speaks out his thoughts aloud, or frankly gives information to the audience – without seeming unnatural and absurd as he would be inclined to do in the modern theatre. Not, however, that the Elizabethans were more disposed than modern audiences to believe in asides or soliloquies as true to life. On the contrary, they accepted such things in full consciousness of their artificiality as being dramatic conventions, that is customs of theatrical presentation, convenient ways of making a certain kind of communication possible between actor and audience. These conventions were effective even though the audience understood very well that such things did not happen in day-to-day reality. Other examples are Oberon's assumption of invisibility by simply saying 'I am invisible', which has already been mentioned, and the custom of stage-disguise illustrated by Rosalind, the heroine of *As You Like It*, who, when dressed up as the boy Ganymede, becomes supposedly unrecognisable even to her own father. Such conventions were the rules of the Elizabethan dramatic game with which the audience were quite familiar, and which they tacitly agreed to accept when they entered the theatre.

The style of acting adopted in the Elizabethan theatre may also have been much more conventional than that of the modern theatre. A modern actor is trained to think himself into the mind of the character he is acting and to adopt the tone of voice and gestures which he thinks such a character would use if he existed as an actual person. Careful choice of appropriate dress and realistic make-up complete this elaborate pretence. An Elizabethan actor was also dressed with great care, though not necessarily in a way that would seem appropriate by modern standards. Theseus, for example, would probably have resembled a gorgeously dressed Elizabethan nobleman rather than a Greek warrior-king. But the purpose of the actor – whatever the nature of his part – would have been above all else to deliver his words in a resounding voice which would do justice to their poetic expressiveness. The language would come first, and the expression of character second. With such an approach to acting it would not, of course, seem odd that the imaginary personages on the stage should speak in verse, which especially in Shakespeare's earlier comedies was often intricately rhymed, and that they should from time to time break into song. This, too, was a convention gladly accepted by the audience for the heightening of their own enjoyment of the play. If a modern equivalent is sought for it is more likely to be found among opera-goers, or the audience of a musical comedy, than among audiences in what is called the 'straight theatre'.

Love was the central theme of many of these plays, but love, too, was governed in its presentation by convention. It was more a matter of words than of passionate embraces and long, lingering kisses. Indeed, this is an instance where attempted realism of the modern kind would itself have been an absurdity in the conditions of the Elizabethan theatre. There were no actresses on the stage, all the female parts were taken by boys whose voices had not yet broken, and, though many of them were accomplished performers at a very early age, there was inevitably a limit to the sexual conviction they might carry. Shakespeare seems to be glancing at this when, in *Antony and Cleopatra,* he makes the boy-actor who plays the part of Cleopatra, the magnificently sensual Queen of Egypt, mock himself by exclaiming,

> *and I shall see*
> *Some squeaking Cleopatra boy my greatness,*
> *I' th' posture of a whore.*

(V.2.218–20)

But, once again, what at first seems a disadvantage is turned to gain, for in *Antony and Cleopatra* passion is converted into words, and these evoke an imaginative response which is more deeply stirring than amorous gestures could ever be.

In *A Midsummer Night's Dream* love is presented comically. The audience are deliberately invited to laugh at the extravagance of Lysander and Demetrius, bemused by the magic love-juice in the wood, and at the bewilderment of Hermia and Helena; and both the words and the gestures of Titania, who wreathes her arms around the ass-headed Bottom (in Act IV, Scene 1, for example), are intentionally absurd. The boy-actors taking these female roles were in no danger of appearing inappropriately ridiculous; and since, in fact, the strongest feelings of all the lovers, both male and female, are more often expressed in squabbles than in loving endearments, it is no disadvantage to have such characters as Titania, Hermia and Helena played by boys. Indeed, since it is the boyishness of young women which Shakespeare is inclined to emphasise here, and elsewhere in his comedies (notably in *As You Like It* where the heroine, Rosalind, dresses up as a boy, and then pretends to play at being a girl), it may be considered a positive advantage to have the female roles taken by boys.

A note on the text

There are few problems with the text of *A Midsummer Night's Dream.* The first printed text is that of 1600. This is one of the 'good' quartos, that is, a text which was issued before the First Folio collected edition of Shakespeare's plays in 1623. It was authorised by the playwright, or the company for which he worked, and was probably printed from the original manuscript. ('Bad' quartos are texts which were pirated by a renegade actor, or a member of the audience, who made a copy from memory and sold it surreptitiously to a printer). There is a second quarto, also dated 1600, but in fact published in 1619. The third printing was that of the 1623 First Folio. For those interested, textual differences, which are not in the main very significant, can be found in the Variorum edition of the play, edited by H. H. Furness (1895), or listed at the end of the Penguin edition, edited by Stanley Wells (1967).

The text of *A Midsummer Night's Dream* to which references are made in these notes is that to be found in the Alexander Edition of *William Shakespeare, The Complete Works,* edited by Peter Alexander (Collins, London and Glasgow, 1951).

Part 2

Summaries
of A MIDSUMMER NIGHT'S
DREAM

A general summary

The action of the play moves from Athens in Act I, to 'a wood near
Athens' for most of Acts II–IV, and back to Athens in Act V. This
movement corresponds with a symbolic change from daylight,
associated with being awake and with reason and common sense; to
night-time, associated with dreaming and irrationality and absurdity;
and back to daylight once more.

Four plots, or groups of characters, are woven together: (1) the
wedding of Theseus and Hippolyta: (2) the love-adventures of
Lysander, Demetrius, Hermia and Helena; (3) the quarrel between
Oberon, the King of the Fairies, and Titania, his Queen; and (4) the
comic business of Bottom and the Athenian workmen, who rehearse
and then perform the play of 'Pyramus and Thisby' as an entertainment at the wedding of Theseus and Hippolyta. Each of these four
plots is of equal importance. In this respect *A Midsummer Night's
Dream* differs from the rest of Shakespeare's comedies, where there is
usually a main plot and one or more sub-plots. Here each plot,
though concerned with sharply contrasted characters and different
kinds of dramatic action, carries as much weight as the others.
Shakespeare's skill is shown both by the way in which he makes use of
the splendid variety afforded by a mixture of plots and by the way he
succeeds in linking one plot with another.

The story of the young lovers connects with that of Theseus and
Hippolyta through Egeus' demand that Theseus, as Duke of Athens
and chief administrator of the law, should help him to impose his
choice of a husband on his daughter, Hermia. Egeus complains that
Lysander has won Hermia's affections and so made her unwilling to
marry another suitor, called Demetrius, who in Egeus' opinion is the
better man. Theseus explains to Hermia that she must obey her father,
or, if not, either die or become a nun. To escape the severity of the
Athenian law Lysander and Hermia make a secret plan to run away together, but allow their friend Helena to know of it. Helena, however,
in love with Demetrius, but spurned by him, betrays them to
Demetrius, who resolves to pursue them, and she herself goes after
Demetrius. Thus all four make their way to the neighbouring wood.

Once in the wood the lovers' fate becomes entwined with that of the fairies. Oberon, wishing to help Helena to win the love of Demetrius, orders his fairy lieutenant, Puck, to apply the juice of a magic flower to the sleeping Demetrius' eyes so that when he wakes he will fall in love with Helena. Puck, however, mistakes Lysander for Demetrius with the result that it is Lysander who is made to change his affection, abandoning Hermia for Helena. Discovering Puck's mistake, Oberon uses the magic juice on Demetrius to make him also love Helena, to the bewilderment and anger of both the young women, and causing jealous strife between the two young men. Eventually magic is again used to undo Lysander's love for Helena and return it to Hermia. The four lovers being now correctly paired, they return to Athens and are married on the same day that Theseus has appointed for his own wedding with Hippolyta, a link with the Bottom plot being achieved in that the newly-weds now form the audience for the workmen's presentation of 'Pyramus and Thisby'.

Through the magic love-juice a connection is also made between the Bottom plot and that of the fairies. Oberon, jealous that Titania will not allow him to have her cherished Indian boy to serve as his page, gains revenge by using his magic to cause her to fall in love with some ugly, monstrous shape. The monster proves to be Bottom ridiculously transformed by Puck into a creature with the head of an ass and the body of a man. To Titania he becomes an 'angel', both 'wise' and 'beautiful', and under the influence of this ridiculous infatuation she forgets her Indian boy, letting him go to Oberon. Having succeeded in his purpose, Oberon restores Titania to her proper senses and Bottom to his normal human shape.

The link between the fairies and Theseus and Hippolyta is less obvious. It is hinted at, however, in the suggestion (at II.1.68–80) that Oberon has in the past had some kind of love relationship with Hippolyta and that Theseus has been led astray by Titania; and, of course, it is through the fairies that the lovers are paired off in such a way that Theseus is relieved of the unpleasant task of passing judgement on Hermia. Moreover, at the end of the play Oberon and Titania, now reunited, dance in Theseus' palace and bless the offspring who are to be born from the triple marriages of Theseus/Hippolyta, Lysander/Hermia and Demetrius/Helena.

Detailed summaries

Act I Scene 1

Theseus and Hippolyta open the play by looking forward to their wedding day ('our nuptial hour'), timed for the appearance of the new moon, and Theseus orders the celebrations to be prepared. Egeus enters with Hermia, Lysander and Demetrius, accusing Lysander of having stolen his daughter's heart and having made her unwilling to marry Demetrius, the man whom Egeus has chosen to be her husband. Egeus claims that by the law of Athens his daughter must either obey him or be put to death. Theseus tries to persuade Hermia that she must accept her father's command, but when pressed by her to say what is the worst that will happen if she refuses, he adds an alternative to the death penalty, namely that she may vow chastity and live shut away from men for the rest of her life in a nunnery. He gives her until the day of his wedding with Hippolyta to make her decision. Lysander protests that he is as worthy a husband as Demetrius, or worthier, since his love is returned by Hermia, whereas Demetrius is inconstant, having previously made love to Helena. Theseus makes his exit saying that he has private advice to give to Egeus and Demetrius. Left alone together Lysander and Hermia lament the crosses which true lovers always suffer, but then Lysander proposes that they should elope to his aunt's house which is far enough away to be beyond the scope of 'the sharp Athenian law'. There they will marry. Hermia agrees, and swears to meet him at an appointed place in the wood outside Athens. At this point Helena enters, wishing that she had the appearance of Hermia, since Hermia is so attractive to Demetrius. Lysander and Hermia tell her that they intend to run away, and, as they go off, wish her better luck with Demetrius. Helena soliloquises on the blindness of love, and ends by saying that she will tell Demetrius of Hermia's flight.

COMMENTARY: The opening is lyrical, giving a romantic atmosphere to the play which is to follow – a comedy of love. Marriage is in the offing, and so this is not a time for sadness: 'Turn melancholy forth to funerals' (line 14), says Theseus. But Theseus also admits that, before the play began, he had conquered Hippolyta by force (lines 16–17), and Egeus' entrance makes us aware that strife and unhappiness are not merely things of the past. He comes 'full of vexation' (line 22), accusing Lysander of having 'bewitch'd' (line 27) Hermia. The accusation is biased; we quickly realise that Egeus is a domineering and possessive father (for example, twice in this scene he insists that Hermia is a kind of property which he owns: 'As she is mine I may dispose of her' and 'she is mine; and all my right of her/I do estate unto Demetrius', lines 42 and 97–8). But the Elizabethans had greater respect for a father's authority than we do today and would probably think that he had some right on his side. Hermia is a young woman following her passions; Egeus an older, more experienced man, and therefore, in Elizabethan eyes, more likely to judge calmly and reasonably. Theseus seems to take this view when he tells Hermia: 'Rather your eyes must with his judgement look' (line 57), and he warns her of the dangers of passion. Later, however, when he tells Egeus and Demetrius that he has some private advice for them, we are given a hint that he does not altogether agree with Egeus. There are two sides to this dispute: the right of a woman to choose her husband according to her fancy, and the right of a father to guide and control his daughter's conduct. The essential thing in this first scene is not to decide which right is the stronger, but to recognise that there is real conflict; and, especially since the death penalty is mentioned, to recognise that this conflict may involve serious suffering. The comedy of love, then, is not going to be so smooth as Theseus' opening words had suggested.

This theme – the suffering which may be involved in a story of love – is taken up by Lysander and Hermia when they are left to occupy the stage alone. It is summed up in the much quoted line: 'The course of true love never did run smooth' (line 134), and the following lines spell out in detail some of the frustrating misfortunes to which love is subject. At this point the tone becomes almost tragic, and many readers have felt a similarity to the love tragedy, *Romeo and Juliet,* which Shakespeare wrote at much the same date as *A Midsummer Night's Dream,* especially in the line, 'So quick bright things come to confusion' – where 'confusion' suggests, not simply 'muddle', but 'chaos and catastrophe'. But Shakespeare does not allow this suggestion to go too far. In the speech beginning, 'I have a widow aunt . . .' (line 157), Lysander puts forward a practical plan to remedy his and Hermia's situation, which Hermia readily accepts, adding some very pretty lovers' oaths ('I swear to thee by Cupid's strongest bow,/By his best arrow . . .' etc., lines 169–78) to assure Lysander that she will keep faith with him. With these oaths the verse also changes. From the beginning of the scene to line 170 it is unrhymed, but now it breaks into rhymed couplets; and it continues in couplets till the end of the scene. This rhyme gives a neat and slightly artificial sound to what the characters say, so that we do not take them too seriously. And this, too, like Lysander's practical proposal for running away from Athens, helps to pull the comedy back from the brink of tragedy.

With Helena's entrance we have another form of lovers' distress. She is unhappy because she is despised by the man she loves, and since that man loves Hermia she wishes (though it is futile to do so) that she had Hermia's beauty. The pun on 'fair' (lines 180–2) rubs in Helena's sense of frustration, but is also slightly silly. Helena, as is apparent from other scenes, is tall and fair, distinguishing her from Hermia who is short and dark, so that 'fair Helena' means both 'fair-haired' and 'beautiful'. But 'fair', to Helena, is only what Demetrius thinks beautiful, therefore it is Hermia who is 'fair', even though she has dark hair, and while Helena herself is not fair. There is also something a little ridiculous in Helena's wishing she could 'catch' Hermia's appearance, voice, eye and tongue, as one catches a sickness (lines 186–9), and in the pit-pat exchanges between her and Hermia at lines 194–201. For example, when Hermia referring to Demetrius, says, 'The more I hate, the more he follows me', Helena replies with an opposite statement, but using the same formula, 'The more I love, the more he hateth me'. She thus expresses something which is truly distressing to her, but in a form of words which make it sound almost like a witty retort. All of which allows us to sympathise with Helena, but ensures that we do not take her grief too seriously.

Helena's wish to exchange her appearance for Hermia's leads on to the final speech of the scene (lines 226–51). This soliloquy (a speech made by a character alone on the stage) dwells on the fantastic changes which are effected by love:

Things base and vile, holding no quantity,
Love can transpose to form and dignity.
Love looks not with the eyes, but with the mind;
And therefore is wing'd Cupid painted blind.

(lines 232–5)

Under Cupid's influence, as Helena says, people fall in love, not with real beauty or real merit, but with imaginary qualities: looking 'with the eyes' stands for seeing people as they actually are, looking 'with the mind' for endowing them with features which they do not possess, but which the infatuated lover wishes to believe that they possess.

In this peculiar emotional condition a lover may give beauty and dignity to what he, or she, would normally regard as ugly and worthless. Love, in other words, has the power to change the aspect of ordinary reality, and it usually does this quite irrationally. Helena, though under love's influence herself, is yet able to understand that Demetrius' present love for Hermia is not necessarily based on any rational judgement that Hermia is a more beautiful or better person than herself. Indeed, she remembers the time when Demetrius swore that he could love no one but her; and this perhaps gives her some faint hope that his love might change again. Be this as it may, her speech is the most important in the play so far, because it alerts us to the unreliable nature of love, and, above all, makes us aware of the strange transformations which love can bring about. We are thus subtly prepared for what is to come later, the most remarkable transformation of all, when Bottom acquires the head of an ass, and yet is adored by the Queen of the Fairies, Titania.

NOTES AND GLOSSARY:

stol'n the impression of her fantasy: imposed upon her imagination, made her fall in love with him

gawds:	toys, trifling things
conceits:	fanciful knick-knacks
blood:	passion, the irrational forces in the human mind
Diana:	goddess of chastity
schooling:	advice, teaching (with a suggestion of rebuke)
cross:	adversity, frustration
collied:	dark
Cupid:	boy-god of love, son of Venus. He is usually represented as an archer whose arrows cause men and women to fall in love, and he has his eyes blindfolded to signify that he takes no account of merit or reason (see lines 235–41)
Venus:	goddess of love. Her chariot is drawn by doves
Carthage Queen:	Dido. She fell in love with Aeneas ('the false Troyan', line 174) and when he deserted her committed suicide on a funeral pyre
translated:	changed. (Compare III.1.109, where Quince exclaims on seeing Bottom transformed with the ass's head. 'Bless thee, Bottom, bless thee! Thou art translated!')
Phoebe:	goddess of the moon

Act I Scene 2

The Athenian workmen – Quince, the carpenter, Bottom, the weaver, Snug, the joiner, Flute, the bellows-mender, Snout, the tinker, and Starveling, the tailor – assemble under Quince's direction to cast the play of 'Pyramus and Thisby', which they intend to put on for the Duke's wedding. Bottom, however, soon asserts his dominance, telling Quince how he should proceed, giving an exhibition of his acting ability by reciting some lines from an old-fashioned tyrant's role, and, though allocated the part of Pyramus, claiming that he could also play the parts of Thisby and the lion. He is confined to Pyramus, however; the rest of the parts are distributed; and Quince tells the actors to meet for rehearsals in the wood.

COMMENTARY: There is a complete contrast in atmosphere between this scene and the first. It is written in prose, following the Elizabethan dramatic convention that noble characters speak verse, and humbler ones prose. In attempting to put on a play these workmen are obviously doing something of which they have very little understanding and no experience. They have simple, naive ideas about drama, as shown by Quince's anxiety that if the lion were to roar too fiercely he would frighten the ladies, and Bottom's prompt reassurance that he would, in fact, do it 'as gently as any sucking dove' (line 73). They also make the typical mistakes of uneducated men trying to use words with which they are not familiar. Thus, Bottom says 'I will aggravate my voice' (line 73), when he means the opposite, and 'obscenely' (line 95) instead of 'seemly'. 'Obscenely', of course, suggests something bawdy and links with the coarse sexual joke in lines 85–6: 'Some of your French crowns have no hair at all'.

The comedy is thus of a vulgar, farcical kind, throwing into relief the more refined atmosphere and sharper tensions of the previous scene. But there are connections as well as contrasts. The laughable contradiction of the title, 'The most Lamentable Comedy and most Cruel Death of Pyramus and Thisby', reminds us of the tragic elements which are nonetheless not to be taken too seriously in Scene 1. This play-within-a-play is clearly going to be a tragedy turned into a farce by the ignorance of its actors, and as such it will be quite appropriate to *A Midsummer Night's Dream* as a comedy which has painful elements within it, while yet remaining comic.

NOTES AND GLOSSARY:

Ercles: Bottom's vulgar version of 'Hercules', a hero of exceptional strength who after his death became a god. Bottom is probably alluding to a well-recognised figure of popular drama, a part which gave the actor plenty of scope for ranting and raving

Phibbus: Phoebus Apollo, god of the sun. As with 'Ercles' for 'Hercules', Bottom gives a vulgar mispronunciation of the name

French crowns: this is a pun on 'crown' = the old French coin, 'écu', and 'crown' = 'head'. Hairlessness was associated with venereal disease, held to be prevalent in France

con: learn

hold, or cut bow-strings: I'll keep my word, or you can write me off (like an archer who has had the string of his bow cut), that is, I'll certainly be there

Act II Scene 1

It is night in the wood near Athens. Puck meets a fairy who serves Titania. He describes the quarrel between Oberon and the Queen over the Indian boy. His own mischievous nature is described by the fairy, and he adds some examples of the practical jokes he likes to play. Oberon and Titania enter from opposite sides of the stage and taunt each other with having had affairs respectively with Hippolyta and Theseus. Titania in a lengthy speech describes the evil influence of their quarrelling thus on the natural world and the seasons. Oberon demands the Indian boy, but Titania refuses, telling how she cherishes the boy for his mother's sake. After Titania's exit Oberon instructs Puck to fetch the magic love-juice flower, the origin of which he describes in an elaborately poetic speech. He will use this juice to gain revenge on Titania. He will drop it into her eyes while she is sleeping, and when she awakes it will cause her to fall in love with the first thing she sees, no matter how repulsive it is. At this point Demetrius, now arrived in the wood in pursuit of Lysander and Hermia, appears on the scene, followed by Helena, and Oberon makes himself invisible so that he can overhear their talk. Demetrius is impatient with Helena, and he tries to drive her away from him by threats of violence; but when he goes off Helena still follows him. Oberon vows to reverse this situation by making Demetrius dote on Helena. When Puck returns with the magic flower, Oberon says that he will use some of it on Titania, and some of it he tells Puck to use so that a certain 'disdainful youth' will fall in love with the lady who loves him, but is at present despised. Oberon says that Puck will know the youth 'by the Athenian garments he hath on', not realising that there is a second Athenian in the wood who might be mistaken for Demetrius. The scene closes with Oberon ordering Puck to meet him again before dawn.

COMMENTARY: This scene takes place at night, a point which, in the absence of lighting effects, is conveyed by the language used, such as Puck's 'The King doth keep his revels here to-night' (line 18), Oberon's 'Ill met by moonlight' (line 60), and Demetrius' warning to Helena that she risks her virginity by trusting 'the opportunity of night' and her reply, 'It is not night when I do see your face' (line 221). And this is not only a question of time. Night creates an atmosphere of magic, uncertainty and mystery, as suggested by the references to Oberon and Titania's meeting by 'spangled starlight' (line 29), or Theseus' being led by Hippolyta 'through the glimmering night' (line 77), or Titania's talking with the Indian boy's mother 'in the spiced Indian air, by night' (line 124).

It is in this special atmosphere that the fairies exist; they are super-natural beings who have powers denied to 'human mortals' of the day-light world, and in this scene where we are first introduced to them we learn something of what they are and what they can do. Puck, for example, can play pranks on other creatures by changing himself into various shapes, distracting a stallion by neighing like a young mare (lines 45–6), or making an old woman spill her ale by lurking in her cup in the shape of a crab-apple (lines 47–50), and as a messenger he can fly with magical speed: 'I'll put a girdle round about the earth/In forty minutes' (lines 175–6). ('Forty', however, is not to be taken literally; it simply means that Puck could fly round the world, if need be, in a very short space of time.) Oberon can make himself invisible (line 186); he has powers of vision which enable him to see the god Cupid 'flying between the cold moon and the earth' (line 156); and he knows the magical properties of herbs and how to use them, (a power which is essential to the story of the play). But, more than this, his account of the origin of the love-juice (lines 148–72) becomes an opportunity to stir the minds of the audience to a sense of wonder. He begins by referring to a mermaid (herself a strange, mythical creature, half woman, half fish) who sings a song of such ravishing harmony that it tames the stormy sea and causes shooting-stars to race through the sky. He then refers to Cupid, who is said to have tried in vain to shoot one of his love-producing arrows into the heart of a 'fair vestal' enthroned in the west. This is usually taken as a compliment to the virgin Queen Elizabeth whose hand was sought in marriage by several royal suitors, but who resisted them all. If so, it lends further majesty and dignity to Oberon's account. (Notice, for example, the splendid ring of 'the imperial vot'ress passed on,/In maiden meditation, fancy-free', lines 163–4.) The arrow falls, instead, on 'a little western flower' which it changes from white to purple, symbolising the pain which love makes lovers feel. 'Love-in-idleness' (now known as the pansy) is the apt name of this flower, but though it is quite a commonplace English flower, Oberon's elaborate story of its origin has taken away its humble, familiar qualities and given it new, imaginatively exciting associations which make it part of the exotic fairy world.

Both Oberon and Titania have great influence on the proper work-ing of nature. Because of their quarrel, as shown by Titania's re-markable speech beginning, 'These are the forgeries of jealousy' (lines 81–117), disorder and turbulence have spread throughout the natural world. Floods, says Titania, have made the rivers overflow their banks, the sodden ground become unfit for the plough, the corn has rotted before it has become ripe, crows feed on the disease-ridden sheep, the countrymen's game called 'nine men's morris' is choked up with mud, and because the mazes can no longer be trodden their paths are overgrown (lines 88–100). Human beings are likewise deprived of the normal pleasures of winter, the damp air causes coughs and colds, and because of this lack of order we see the seasons turned upside down: new-blown roses are attacked by frost, and on Winter's frail and icy head, as if to mock him, is set a coronet of sweet summer buds (lines 101–11). Spring, summer, autumn and winter are all confused, and the bewildered world cannot tell the seasons by their products (lines 111–14). And, concludes Titania, all of these evils are the offspring of our quarrelling (referring to herself and Oberon).

As this speech shows, however, the special qualities and mysterious powers of the fairies do not make them totally separate and remote from human beings. Their actions, after all, do have important effects on ordinary, day-to-day life, and their own behaviour is not unlike that of human beings. For all their dignity as King and Queen of the fairies, when Oberon and Titania quarrel they display emotions very much like those of ordinary jealous men and women. We are also about to see Titania subjected to the same transforming effect of love as Helena had described in her soliloquy at the end of Act I Scene 1. Her statement that 'Things base and vile, holding no quantity,/Love can transpose to form and dignity' is echoed in Oberon's prophecy that when the love-juice is dropped in the sleeping Titania's eyes,

> *The next thing then she waking looks upon,*
> *Be it on lion, bear, or wolf, or bull,*
> *On meddling monkey, or on busy ape,*
> *She shall pursue it with the soul of love.*

(lines 179–82)

Fairy love can thus be influenced by the same absurd forces as human love; and when a few lines later Demetrius enters, distraught because he cannot find Hermia, followed by Helena, distraught because Demetrius will have nothing to do with her, we feel that there is a common bond of irrationality between them and the fairies. Demetrius' line, 'And here am I, and wood within this wood' (line 192), with its pun on 'wood' = 'mad' and 'wood' = 'forest', sums it up for us. The wood, especially at night, is a place where love, at odds with common sense and reason, can most readily effect its strange transformations, on human beings and fairies alike. At the same time wood, night and powers which transcend those of ordinary human beings belong quite naturally with the fairies. Mystery and unreason, that is to say, are two sides of the same coin. Together they make up the 'dream' world of *A Midsummer Night's Dream*.

NOTES AND GLOSSARY:

pensioners:	body-guard (not as in the modern meaning)
lob:	clown
square:	quarrel
And 'tailor' cries:	the old woman cries, either 'Thief', or 'That brings me down on my tail'. Either way, it is an undignified cry of annoyance
Corin and Phillida:	typical names in conventional love pastoral (poetry supposedly concerned with shepherds and shepherdesses)
the bouncing Amazon:	Hippolyta
Perigouna, Aegles, Ariadne and **Antiopa:**	all maidens supposedly seduced by the amorous Theseus
continents:	banks
Hiems:	winter
Neptune:	god of the sea
leviathan:	whale
adamant:	magnetic stone
Apollo and Daphne:	Apollo fell in love with the nymph, Daphne, who fled from him and was changed into a laurel
griffin:	monster with the body of a lion and head of an eagle. As with Apollo and Daphne in line 231, the normal roles are reversed
weed:	dress

Act II Scene 2

Titania enters with her fairy followers. She asks them to sing her to sleep with a song, which they do, and then leave her alone. Oberon makes a brief appearance to drop the love-juice in her eyes, and goes out again. (This probably takes place in the inner stage – see Introduction, page 11.) Lysander and Hermia enter next (to the main stage). They have lost their way in the wood, and since Hermia is tired they decide to sleep for a while, Hermia insisting, however, for modesty's sake, that Lysander lies down at some distance from her. Puck finds them asleep, and, mistaking Lysander for Demetrius, puts some of the love-juice on his eyes. After Puck's exit Demetrius and Helena come running on to the stage, though Demetrius quickly escapes from Helena. Seeing Lysander lying on the ground (but missing Hermia), Helena wakes him with her cry of alarm. Because of the magic juice he immediately falls in love with her. Helena, however, merely thinks that he is making fun of her, and departs. Lysander, now expressing contempt for the still-sleeping Hermia, also departs in pursuit of Helena. Immediately afterwards Hermia starts up, calling on Lysander for help, as she has just had a dream in which it seemed to her that a serpent was eating her heart away, while Lysander sat by smiling. On finding that Lysander has disappeared, she is terrified and goes off to look for him.

COMMENTARY: The opening of this scene creates more fairy atmosphere through Titania's instructions to her followers to kill the larvae which blight roses and to capture bats' wings to make coats for her elves – all in 'the third part of a minute' (line 2), the shortness of which suggests how swift fairy movements must be. The song, which, as so often in Shakespearean comedy, adds to the variety of the audience's entertainment, suggests that her followers will protect Titania while she is sleeping, but we already know that

> *Never harm*
> *Nor spell nor charm*
> *Come our lovely lady nigh*   (lines 16–18)

is likely to prove to be in vain.

The rest of the scene is mainly swift action, one set of entrances and exits rapidly succeeding another in a way that keeps the audience very interested in what will happen next. But the theme of the irrationality of love is also kept going. Lysander, for example, fervently assures Hermia that she may safely allow him to lie down close to her because they are two persons made one by their mutual vows of love, and 'lying so, Hermia, I do not lie' (line 52), that is, he does not tell a lie. As soon as he is woken by Helena, however, he declares himself utterly dedicated to her. When reminded about Hermia he argues that his previous love was immature, and now 'reason' says to him that Helena is 'the worthier maid' (line 116). 'Reason' is, in fact, mentioned four times within the space of six lines (115–20), but the more he talks of reason the more the audience, being aware of the true cause of his change of heart, knows that he is merely finding apparently rational excuses for his quite irrational emotions. Towards the end of the scene, indeed, he goes to the opposite extreme and seems now to hate Hermia more fervently than he had previously loved her. This, of course, is laughably extravagant in the eyes of the audience, but the very last lines of the scene are a reminder that it is one thing to be an onlooker at the comedy of love, but quite another thing to be a participant. Hermia is genuinely distressed to find herself deserted. She does not yet know that her lover has stopped loving her, but her dream of the serpent has aroused deep, inexplicable anxiety. We, the audience, know that her dream has a kind of truth. We feel for her; and we perhaps reflect that, paradoxical though it may seem, 'reason' in this scene is less to be trusted than dreaming.

NOTES AND GLOSSARY:

rere-mice: bats
Philomel: the nightingale
ounce: lynx
Pard: leopard
darkling: in the dark
fond: foolish
sphery eyne: eyes which are as bright as stars
Transparent: beautiful, brightly shining, pure
gentleness: nobility

Act III Scene 1

Titania still sleeps at the back of the stage. Bottom and the other Athenian workmen enter, and Quince declares this a good place for their rehearsal of 'Pyramus and Thisby'. Bottom objects that Pyramus' drawing a sword to kill himself will frighten the ladies in their audience, but he suggests the writing of a prologue to be spoken before the performance which will explain that Pyramus does not die, and that he is really Bottom the weaver. Snout asks if the ladies would not also be afraid of the lion. To remedy this Bottom suggests that Snug's face should be shown through the lion's neck, and that he should reassure the ladies by speaking to them and telling them who he is. The further supposed difficulties of providing moonlight and a wall are resolved by having one of the actors enter with a bush of thorns (traditionally associated with the imaginary figure of the man in the moon) and a lantern to represent moonshine, and another actor covered with builder's material such as plaster, loam (a mixture of sand and clay) or roughcast (plaster and small stones) who will hold up his fingers to represent the hole through which Pyramus and Thisby may speak. As the workmen begin their rehearsal, Puck creeps in behind, and resolves to listen to them, and play an active part, too, if he sees opportunity for fun. The rehearsal goes forward with the actors making various ridiculous mistakes. When Bottom, as Pyramus in the play-within-a-play, makes an exit, he is followed by Puck, who, we are to understand, transforms him so that when Bottom re-enters (at line 92) he has on an ass's head. This scares the rest of the workmen into headlong flight, further bewildered and terrified by Puck, who uses his magical powers to make himself appear to them as horse, hound, hog, headless bear or a flame of fire, and to make them scratch themselves on bushes and briars. Snout and Quince make momentary reappearances to tell Bottom that he is 'translated', but he remains unaware of what has happened to him, suspecting his workmates of merely trying to play some practical joke on him. To show that he is not afraid he sings a song, which wakes Titania from her sleep, and since the first thing she sees is Bottom she immediately falls in love with him. She offers him her fairies to wait on him (though she also uses her power to prevent him from leaving the wood), and summoning Peaseblossom, Cobweb, Moth and Mustardseed she tells them to fetch various delightful, but quite inappropriate, things to entertain Bottom. Bottom himself then speaks to each fairy in turn, and makes requests more in keeping with his own tastes. Titania tells her fairies to lead him to her bower, and finishes with 'Tie up my love's tongue, bring him silently'.

COMMENTARY: At first this scene strikes one as being simply a highly comic collision of the gross with the refined, and of prosaic, literal-minded workmen with fairies, creatures of folklore and the poetic imagination. The workmen's misgivings about the disturbing effect which their play might have on the ladies is evidence of how little they understand the nature of dramatic illusion and the work of the imagination. They think that a play will deceive its audience into taking it for reality, and also, of course, they have an amusingly false confidence in their own ability to make 'Pyramus and Thisby' convincingly true to life. They speak in prose and they have prose minds, unable to appreciate how poetry works. Puck realises this, and he quickly thinks of them as apt subjects for the sort of practical jokes he loves to play (compare his account of himself at II.1.43–57). His putting of an ass's head on Bottom is almost a representation of the stupidity which he thinks this particular workman embodies.

However, the fairies do not have it all their own way. Titania is undoubtedly, as she herself claims, 'a spirit of no common rate' (line 140), but the dignified impression she creates is undercut in this very scene by her ridiculous exclamation: 'What angel wakes me from my flowry bed? (line 128), and her saying to Bottom, 'Thou art as wise as thou art beautiful' (line 135). If she can be so utterly mistaken, what does this suggest about her own wisdom and refinement? (For that matter, what does Puck's behaviour suggest about his sense of humour?) She is, of course, under the influence of magic, and so not behaving normally.

Bottom, on the other hand, is not quite the ass that he literally appears to be. The audience laughs *at* him when, unconscious of his own appearance, he says 'this is to make an ass of me' (line 110), but we laugh both *at* and *with* him when, without seeming unduly put out, or disconcerted, he accepts his position, strange though it is, as Titania's lover, and manages to be courteous to the fairies who offer him their services at Titania's command. He does not seem particularly interested in such things as honey bags stolen from humble bees, but it must be admitted that he thinks of good practical uses for cobwebs (which were used to stop bleeding) and for mustard (that is, to eat with beef). He is especially sensible in the comment he makes on Titania's declaration of love: 'Methinks, mistress, you should have little reason for that. And yet, to say the truth, reason and love keep little company together now-a-days' (lines 130–3). This reference to reason is far more rational than the 'reason' on which Demetrius insisted in Act II Scene 2. It is, in fact, a very appropriate comment, not only on Bottom's own situation, but on what is happening throughout *A Midsummer Night's Dream*. From this point of view Bottom is indeed 'wise' – with the wisdom of the fool, who often speaks better sense than those who are supposed to be wiser than he.

NOTES AND GLOSSARY:

tiring-house:	dressing-room
By'r lakin:	by Our Lady (the Virgin Mary), an oath
eight and six:	verse consisting of a line of eight syllables followed by one of six
hempen homespuns:	coarse rustics (who might be expected to wear home-made cloth of hemp)
ousel:	blackbird
cuckoo:	the sound of the cuckoo is associated with cuckolding. The song implies that many a man cannot deny that his wife has been unfaithful, but Bottom misses the meaning
gleek:	jest
Squash:	name derived from the word for an unripe pea-pod
enforced:	violated, raped

Act III Scene 2

Oberon wonders what kind of creature Titania fell in love with, and Puck describes how he put an ass's head on Bottom, causing confusion among the other workmen, and how Titania 'wak'd, and straightway lov'd an ass' (line 34). Puck also says that he has caused 'the Athenian' to fall in love with 'the Athenian woman', but with the entrance of Demetrius still urging love on Hermia Puck's mistake becomes apparent. Hermia, upset because she cannot find Lysander, thinks that Demetrius has jealously done him some harm. She breaks away from Demetrius, who then, overcome with weariness, lies down to sleep. Oberon commands Puck to find Helena and bring her to this spot, while the King himself puts some love-juice in Demetrius' eye. Puck, delighting in the complications which his mistake has brought about, re-enters with the news that Helena is near at hand, followed by Lysander who is begging love from her. Helena still resists Lysander, pointing out that the vows he now makes to her are due to Hermia, to which Lysander replies, 'Demetrius loves her, and he loves not you' (line 136). But no sooner are these words out of Lysander's mouth than Demetrius wakes up and, seeing Helena, exclaims his love for *her*: 'O Helen, goddess, nymph, perfect, divine!' (line 137). Helena's reaction is to think that both men are playing an unkind joke on her, and she protests. Lysander and Demetrius each urge the other to give up Helena. At this point Hermia enters, having been drawn to the spot by the sound of Lysander's voice. She is bewildered to find herself rejected by Lysander, but Helena thinks that Hermia is merely pretending dismay to help the men in their practical joke. For the sake of their old childhood friendship Helena begs Hermia to stop taunting her in this way. Hermia, still amazed, tries to get Lysander to stop professing love to Helena; Demetrius declares that he will not beg, but force Lysander to stop; and soon a quarrel breaks out between the two men, in which Hermia tries to hold Lysander back, but the more she does so, the more Demetrius accuses Lysander of cowardice. Events now convince Hermia that she has indeed lost Lysander's love, and, jumping to the conclusion that this is the other woman's fault, she quarrels with Helena, her anger especially seizing on what she takes to be an insult based on her lack of height compared with Helena. Lysander at last breaks free from Hermia's hold, and he and Demetrius go out together to settle their quarrel by a duel. Hermia blames Helena, probably also making a movement to attack her, but Helena, being the more timid of the two, runs away. Hermia also makes her exit. Oberon, to prevent things getting worse, orders Puck to use his powers of disguise to lead Lysander and Demetrius astray till they fall asleep with weariness, and then to put a new magic juice in Lysander's eyes which will undo the effect of the old one, restoring him to his previous love for Hermia. Meanwhile Oberon will ask for the Indian boy from Titania, and restore her also to her normal state of mind.

Morning is approaching, and though Oberon declares that he and the other fairies are not wicked spirits condemned to range abroad only at night, he nevertheless wants to get everything put right before day. After Oberon's exit, Puck comes in, leading first Lysander, then Demetrius, by making each one mistake him for his opponent. At last both lie down exhausted. Helena and Hermia are then separately brought in, and they too lie down to sleep. Puck squeezes the love-antidote in Lysander's eyes, and promises that 'Jack shall have Jill' (line 461) – all shall be well, and the lovers will be paired off harmoniously.

COMMENTARY: Although the workmen and the young lovers do not actually appear together in this scene, Puck's account of the confusion he caused the workmen in the previous scene links them closely with the confusion caused among the lovers by the effects of the misapplied love-juice. The remarkable image of the wild geese and jackdaws scattering madly into the sky after the hunter has shot his gun (lines 20–4) helps to fix the workmen's sense of bewilderment and confusion in the audience's mind, and the phrase, 'senseless things begin to do them wrong' (line 28), sums up memorably the way in which their 'distracted fear' (line 31) makes them see mere bushes as living creatures snatching at their garments. The lovers do not fall into that particular mistake, but love, in the form of the magic juice, causes illusions just as great and drives them equally distracted. By the end of the scene Lysander and Demetrius are being deceived by Puck's disguises and led in frantic circles, with quite as much extravagance as the workmen, and Helena and Hermia's bewilderment about who loves them and who does not, provides at least a mental equivalent of this physical distraction.

The scene is full of sharp contradictions further emphasising this topsy-turvydom. The comic placing of Demetrius' 'O Helen, goddess, nymph, perfect, divine', so that it exactly contradicts Lysander's immediately preceding line, is one striking example, and the exaggerated language in which he goes on to praise Helena's beauty, ridiculous by its very exaggeration, also suggests qualities which bewilderingly turn into their opposites: Helena's eyes, he says, are so bright that they make perfectly transparent crystal seem mud by comparison – a contrast greatly heightened by the form of the statement, 'crystal is muddy' (line 139), which actually seems to affirm that crystal *is* mud. Likewise, the purest snow on the Taurus range of mountains seems as black as a crow when it is compared with the pure whiteness of Helena's hand – again the actual language heightening the effect because of the phrase '*turns* to a crow' (line 142).

For Helena, too, things seem to be turning into their opposites. She hears Lysander making vows to her that belong by right to Hermia. In such a situation 'Truth' (= 'faithfulness', but with a pun on 'truth' = accuracy or correctness) 'kills truth'; it becomes a contradiction in terms like the phrase 'devilish-holy fray' (line 129). And Helena sees not only Lysander, but Demetrius too, switching allegiances in a most confusing way:·

> *You both are rivals, and love Hermia;*
> *And now both rivals, to mock Helena.*

(lines 155–6)

Likewise, her relationship to Hermia is affected. She dwells at length on their childhood friendship: they were so close that they were a kind of two-in-one, working together on one flower in the same piece of embroidery, sharing the same cushion, and singing the same song in the same key, almost as if they were part of the same body; they were separate and yet grew together like a double cherry, having two bodies, but one heart, as a coat of arms in heraldry may carry the separate arms of man and wife, and yet show them joined together under the same crest (lines 204–14). But now, as Hermia seems to be taking sides with the men against her, it appears to Helena as if this 'ancient love' is being torn in two (line 215), and as if Hermia herself is ceasing to behave like a modest young woman: 'tis not maidenly;/Our sex, as well as I, may chide you for it' (lines 217–18).

The confusion, the contradictions and the anger of all four young people increase in intensity as the scene develops, but at the same time it remains a series of comic mistakes and misunderstandings – 'jangling', in fact, which the mischief-loving Puck esteems 'a sport' (line 353). Moreover, the audience knows that Oberon is there all the time as an onlooker, with the power to put things right, and that therefore the lovers' passions need not cause too much anxiety. And, indeed, after Hermia's exit at line 344, bewildered and knowing 'not what to say', Oberon steps forward to take firm control, issuing the necessary commands to restore order, and indicating that Titania, also, will be released from delusion. When the lovers emerge from their confusion what they have experienced in the woodland night 'Shall seem a dream and fruitless vision' (line 371), and when Titania recovers from her dotage on Bottom 'all things shall be peace' (line 377).

Appropriately, in the latter part of this scene we are given hints that the goddess of dawn is not far off: 'yonder shines Aurora's harbinger' (line 380). The traditional superstitions of the English countryside are evoked (lines 381–7), to suggest that ghosts, for example, and the unhappy spirits of suicides, who were buried at cross-roads, must now go back to their corpses, since they belong only to the darkness and cannot bear the light. Lest the fairies of this play, however, should be associated with such spirits, Oberon is made to say that 'we are spirits of another sort', and to explain that, though they belong chiefly to the night, they are allowed to enjoy the morning, too (lines 388–93). Other hints are also given that dawn and daylight sanity are coming when Demetrius, as he lies down to sleep, utters one last word of defiance to Lysander: 'By day's approach look to be visited' (line 430); when Helena sighs for the morning: 'Shine comforts from the east . . .', (line 432); and when Hermia says she will rest 'till the break of day' (line 446). Finally, a complete assurance of return to daylight normality is given by Puck's 'country proverb' jingle:

> *Jack shall have Jill;*
> *Nought shall go ill;*
> *The man shall have his mare again, artd all shall be well.*

With this the scene ends.

NOTES AND GLOSSARY:

nole: noddle

choughs: jackdaws

sense . . . senseless: pun on two different meanings of 'sense': (1) understanding, common sense; (2) without feeling, inanimate

from yielders all things catch: anything that gives is caught up. (Wells, however, interprets 'yielders' as 'the timid' – see the Penguin edition of *A Midsummer Night's Dream,* p. 145.)

I'll believe . . . th'Antipodes: a fantastic image. The idea is that a tunnel might be made through the centre of the earth to the opposite side where it is day when it is night here. The moon could then creep through the tunnel and displease her brother, the sun, by shining with him at noon

oes and eyes: a double pun. 'Oes' = stars, but also the letter 'O' and the sigh, 'Oh'; 'eyes' = metaphor for stars, the letter 'I' and the sigh, 'Ay'

confederacy: conspiracy

Two of the first . . . one crest: Helena suggests that she and Hermia may have two separate bodies, but they are united as are the two separate coats of arms of a man and a wife when they are quartered together under the same crest to denote their marriage

curst: ill-tempered

minimus: diminutive thing

knot-grass: a spreading weed that trips one up

amaz'd: in a maze, bewildered

welkin: sky

Acheron: one of the rivers of Hades

Aurora: goddess of the dawn

Act IV Scene 1

The scene begins with Titania still doting on Bottom, and Bottom still basking comfortably in his strange situation. He asks Cobweb to fetch a bee's honey-bag for him and Mustardseed to join with Peaseblossom and Cobweb in scratching his head. Titania offers him fairy music, but Bottom chooses the crude rustic music of 'the tongs and the bones'; and the effect of his transformation is seen in his preference for oats, or hay, or dried peas rather than the squirrel's nuts which Titania suggests. When he feels tired Titania holds him in her arms, and they fall asleep. Oberon, who has been watching from behind, now comes forward, greeting Puck, to whom he explains that he now has the Indian boy and therefore intends to release Titania from her enchantment, which he does. Titania then awakes and is disgusted to see what she has loved. Puck is ordered to remove the ass's head; the fairies dance; and Oberon promises to bless the weddings of Theseus and the lovers. As they go out, the sound of hunting horns is heard, and Theseus enters, accompanied by Hippolyta (whom he is to marry this day) and Egeus and followers. Theseus boasts of the music created by the cry of his hounds. He then notices the lovers asleep, and orders his huntsmen to wake them with the sound of the horns. He wonders how it comes about that Lysander and Demetrius, who were previously such enemies, now appear to be friends. Egeus, as at the beginning of the play, demands the fulfilment of the law, but when Demetrius explains that he now loves Helena, Theseus overrules Egeus, and proposes that the lovers shall be married at the same time as Hippolyta and himself. After everyone else has left the stage, Bottom, the one remaining sleeper (who has not been noticed by Theseus or the lovers) awakes. He thinks himself still in the middle of the rehearsal, awaiting his cue, but finds that the other actors have gone. His experience with Titania seems like a marvellous dream, and he decides to get Peter Quince to celebrate it in a ballad.

COMMENTARY: The first part of this scene carries on the comedy of ludicrous contrast between delicate fairies and gross Bottom, but with Bottom showing his native adaptability, which we have already seen at Act III Scene 1. It then moves into the restoration of order which was promised at the end of the immediately preceding scene (that is Act III Scene 3), with Titania regaining her normal senses and becoming 'new in amity' (line 84) with Oberon. The function of the music called for at line 82, and of the dance which is performed to it, is to symbolise this return from discord to harmony, and it is followed by other references to musical concord which include Duke Theseus and the lovers in a similar atmosphere of harmony made all the

sweeter and more welcome by contrast with discord and confusion.
Thus, when Theseus invites Hippolyta to go with him up to the top of a
hill so that they can hear the cry of his hounds echoing in the valley
below he speaks of this sound as a kind of pleasurable mixture of
concord and discord:

> We will, fair Queen, up to the mountain's top,
> And mark the musical confusion
> Of hounds and echo in conjunction.

(lines 106–8)

In reply Hippolyta speaks of the hounds of Hercules and Cadmus
which produced 'so musical a discord' (line 115). Later, when speaking
to the lovers, Theseus is surprised to find such 'gentle concord' (line
140) between 'rival enemies' (line 139), and the renewal of family
strife which is threatened by Egeus' words (lines 151–6) is converted
by Theseus into the prospect of marital harmony and a bond which
'shall eternally be knit' (line 178).

Bottom also has his part in this atmosphere, for his initial sense of
confusion on waking to a rehearsal, as he thinks, from which his fellow-
actors have stolen away, rapidly turns into a sense of wonder at the
'most rare vision' (line 203) which has been vouchsafed to him. In
his excited attempt to express what he feels is inexpressible he falls into
a verbal confusion which is a comic equivalent to Hippolyta's 'so
musical a discord': 'The eye of man hath not heard, the ear of man
hath not seen, man's hand is not able to taste, his tongue to conceive,
nor his heart to report, what my dream was.' Commentators differ
among themselves as to whether these words of Bottom's are an
intentional parody of the Bible's 'The eye hath not seen, and the ear
hath not heard, neither have entered into the heart of man, the
things which God hath prepared for them that love him' (1 Corinthians
2:9). The Elizabethans were so familiar with the Bible that it seems
likely that a parody is intended and would have been easily recognised
by Shakespeare's original audiences; in which case an even greater
comedy of contrast and harmonious discord would be suggested –
the sacred words of scripture being turned upside down by the profane,
but nonetheless harmless, Bottom. Even without this, however,
Bottom's tumbling into verbal contradictions (the eye hearing and the
hand tasting), besides being a simple, popular form of humour,
creates a sense of glorious muddle, belonging appropriately enough to
a character who has always been prone to make verbal mistakes and
who, at this particular moment is still in the slightly befuddled state
between waking and 'dreaming'; and the clash between the grandly
marvellous and the ridiculously commonplace which is suggested by

this 'glorious muddle' may be regarded as a variation on 'musical discord', since it sounds a false note, but creates laughter and delight in the very process of doing so.

Bottom's uncertainty about where he is on first awaking echoes the uncertainty of the lovers when awakened by Theseus' horns. Lysander, for example, who says he is 'half sleep, half waking' (line 144), speaks in broken phrases:

> *I cannot truly say how I came here,*
> *But, as I think – for truly would I speak,*
> *And now I do bethink me, so it is –*
> *I came with Hermia hither.*

(lines 145–8)

And Demetrius and Hermia later speak of the uncertainty of their vision (lines 184–7). Demetrius thinks that perhaps he and the other lovers are still sleeping, still dreaming (line 191); and even when convinced that they are awake, he suggests that they follow Theseus, but on the way tell each other their dreams. This state of uncertainty between waking and sleeping parallels the state between concord and discord already discussed, and also carries on the sense of approaching morning emphasised in Act III Scene 2. We are reminded specifically of that approach by Puck's words:

> *Fairy King, attend and mark;*
> *I do hear the morning lark.*

(lines 90–1)

Shakespeare does not, however, place a simple, uncomplicated emphasis on morning and the waking world of daylight. We may be in the process of returning to the real world of everyday awareness, but the world of vision and dream is not to be banished. This is not, for example, the end of the fairies; Oberon gives a hint that they will return (lines 85–7).

In this connection it is worth paying attention to what Theseus says about his Spartan hounds (lines 116–23). In some ways this is descriptive poetry with a more realistic flavour than that which belongs to the fantastic and highly coloured fairy scenes. The hounds are brought vividly before us as large-jawed and sandy in colour, with ears so long that they sweep the ground and full, heavy dewlaps. They are meant for hunting, and yet the curious thing is that Theseus has had them bred more for the sake of the notes which their varying cries produce, as if they were a peal of bells ranging from tenor to bass, than for the sake of their powers of scent and speed, which are the specifically hunting qualities of hounds. Indeed, he says that they are 'slow in pursuit', though he seems to find their musical qualities ample compensation for this. In other words the aesthetic, *un*-useful qualities of the hounds seem to matter more to him than the useful ones. And yet Theseus seems to be a sensible, practical man, essentially of the daylight world. If Oberon rules in the night, he rules in the day. But just as Oberon can spend some hours in daylight, so Theseus can go outside his practical, daytime world to find pleasure in 'musical confusion' (line 107). We must, then, be prepared in this play not for simple opposition between night and day, but for interpenetration.

NOTES AND GLOSSARY:

neaf: fist

the tongs and the bones: rustic instruments: the 'tongs' were pieces of metal struck by a key, the 'bones' consisted of two bones rattled together between the fingers (as schoolboys do to this day)

peck: an old measure = a quarter of a bushel, or two gallons

exposition: one of Bottom's characteristic mistakes in the use of words. He means 'disposition'

vaward: early part, that is, it is very early morning

So flew'd, so sanded: with the same large jaws, and of the same sandy colour

dew-lapp'd: having loose skin hanging beneath the throat

Saint Valentine: saint associated with love. St Valentine's day = 14 February, a day when lovers choose each other and birds are supposed to choose their mates (hence line 137, 'Begin these wood-birds but to couple now?')

Peradventure: perhaps

Act IV Scene 2

In this short scene, set once more in Athens, the workmen regret that Bottom cannot be found and that therefore, even though their play of 'Pyramus and Thisby' has been chosen to be performed before the Duke, it cannot go forward. But at this point Bottom appears, without the ass's head, and as usual he immediately takes charge, telling everyone to meet at the palace for the performance of the play.

Act V Scene 1

The scene is the palace of Theseus in Athens. The marriages of Theseus and Hippolyta, Lysander and Hermia, and Demetrius and

Helena have already been solemnised, and, as Bottom had mentioned at the end of Act IV, Scene 1 ('the Duke hath dined', line 31), they have had supper. They have been talking of the events in the wood, and the scene opens with Hippolyta referring to these as 'strange' (line 1). Theseus is sceptical and delivers a speech on the deceptions which result from fantasy. The lovers enter and exchange courtesies with Theseus, who then asks Philostrate, the Master of the Revels, what kind of entertainment is available to make the hours between now and bedtime seem short. Among the offerings are a song, to be sung rather inappropriately by a eunuch, about the battle of the Centaurs; a description (or perhaps a sensational dramatisation) of the drunken devotees of Bacchus, the god of wine, tearing the poet-musician Orpheus to pieces; a satirical account of the nine Muses mourning for the death of Learning; and the workmen's play of Pyramus and Thisby. Amused by its paradoxical title, Theseus chooses the workmen's play, despite the discouragement of Philostrate, who dismisses the actors as inept amateurs, and of Hippolyta, who says that it is painful to see people struggling to do something which is quite beyond them. Theseus replies that it is the goodness of the intention that matters, and so the play-within-the-play goes on. Quince enters first as the Prologue, with a speech designed to secure the good will of the audience, which, however, he garbles by putting the punctuation in the wrong places. Then follow Bottom as Pyramus, Flute as Thisby, Snout as Wall, Starveling as Moonshine, and Snug as Lion, performing the play in dumb show while the Prologue recites the plot. All the actors then go out, except for Snout, who explains that he is the Wall, and that his fingers represent the chink through which Pyramus and Thisby are to whisper. The play then begins in its spoken form, interrupted from time to time by witty comments from the stage audience, consisting of Theseus, Hippolyta and the lovers. First enters Pyramus, making exaggerated to-do because he thinks that Thisby has failed to keep her promise to meet him, and next Thisby. They exchange vows of love through the 'wall', and agree to meet at Ninus' tomb. After they go out, so does Snout, saying that Wall has done his bit. Next enter Snug and Starveling. Snug makes his little speech explaining that he is not really a fierce lion, but only harmless Snug, the joiner, and Starveling, somewhat put out by the audience's mocking comments, lamely explains the meaning of his lantern, himself and his thorn-bush and dog. The scene is now supposed to be Ninus' tomb by moonlight. Thisby re-enters, is frightened by 'Lion' and runs off, dropping her mantle as she does so. Lion tears the mantle and makes his exit, too. Pyramus next enters, addresses the moon, finds Thisby's blood-stained mantle, assumes that she is dead, and with ludicrous outcry kills himself. At his words, 'Moon, take thy flight' (line 297),

Starveling goes off, occasioning the mocking comment from Theseus that Thisby will have to find Pyramus' body by starlight. Thisby enters, makes a would-be poetic lament over the body, and stabs herself. Bottom springs up from the 'dead' and offers Theseus an Epilogue or a peasant dance called 'a Bergomask'. The dance is preferred and is performed by the workmen, after which Theseus says it is midnight, time for the lovers to retire to bed. After all have gone, Puck enters with a broom, 'To sweep the dust behind the door' (line 379), followed by Oberon, Titania and the fairies. They sing and dance, and Oberon pronounces a blessing on the marriages which will make them fruitful and protect the offspring which will be born of them from all kinds of disfigurement. Finally, Puck, alone on the stage, speaks to the actual theatre audience and asks for their applause.

COMMENTARY: Theseus' speech at the beginning of this Act takes up that theme of reason and imagination to which frequent reference has been made and gives what is the most emphatic statement of the common-sense, daylight point of view. Theseus is a rational sceptic who distrusts 'antique fables', old-fashioned and outlandish stories, of the kind, no doubt, enshrined in myth, and 'fairy toys', trivial stories about fairies and supernatural beings which cannot be taken seriously. Lovers and madmen alike, he says, are the victims of mental excitement which leads them to imagine they see things which to the cool and rational person are non-existent. Indeed, the lunatic, the lover, and the poet as well, are all made up of imagination: the madman imagines he sees more devils than hell can hold; the lover, equally deluded, thinks he sees the beauty of Helen of Troy in a gypsy's face; and the poet, carried away by a kind of splendid madness, allows his eye to range over the whole span from heaven to earth, and as his imagination gives birth to hitherto unknown beings his writing turns them into verbal shapes, thus giving a name and a recognisable form of existence to that which is as insubstantial as the air. The power of the imagination is so great that it can play strange tricks on man: if it imagines something joyful, it further imagines, and gives the semblance of reality to, some being who will bring that joy into existence; or in the night, when man's fearfulness makes him a prey to illusions, how easily does he mistake a bush for a bear! That concluding couplet

Or in the night, imagining some fear,
How easy is a bush suppos'd a bear?

(lines 21–2)

sums up Theseus' attitude. Imagination belongs to darkness which prevents one from seeing things clearly according to reason, and breeds illusions, which may be terrifying at the time, but which in the daylight, that is in a more rational state of mind, are seen for the ridiculous misconceptions that they really are. But there is also irony in what Theseus says: some of his words convey a meaning which contradicts his own argument. He cannot believe 'these antique fables' (line 3), and yet Theseus himself is for us a mythical hero from 'antique fable', some of whose exploits have already been referred to in the play (for example his conquest of Hippolyta and the Amazons, and the love adventures with Perigouna, Aegles, Ariadne and Antiopa alluded to in II.1.77–80), and later in this same scene he will himself allude to his kinship with the great hero and demi-god, Hercules, and to his conquest of Thebes (lines 46–51). It is also noticeable, that, although he brackets lunatic, lover and poet together, when he elaborates on the imagination of the poet Theseus seems to leave some of his mockery behind. Instead of emphasising the unreality of what the poet does, Theseus grows quite eloquent about the tremendous range of the poet's vision, which glances 'from heaven to earth, from earth to heaven' (line 13), and accords him an almost godlike ability to create something out of nothing. Above all, at the conclusion of Theseus' speech, Hippolyta, to whom it has been addressed, remains unconvinced, for, she says, the lovers' accounts of what has happened in the darkness of the wood seem to tally with each other, and, no matter how strange they may be, they add up to something which has such consistency and truth that it must be believed. In other words, Theseus' level-headed common sense is contradicted by experience, and the audience, having seen the strange things that happen to the lovers, are bound to feel that Hippolyta's argument is a weighty one.

There is a further point, which involves not only this scene, but the entire play which is being staged; indeed, it might be said to involve the nature of drama itself. The audience listening to Theseus' argument on behalf of reason and common sense know quite well that this 'Theseus' is in fact an ordinary actor playing the part created for him by Shakespeare, and that the lovers, fairies and the rest are equally figments of the dramatist's imagination. If Theseus were to carry his point that imagination merely creates discreditable illusions, he would only succeed in discrediting himself, his whole company of fellow-actors and the very play in which they are performing! The truth is that drama depends on the creation of a very special kind of illusion by which the audience are not deceived, but which they accept as 'real' during the time of the performance for the sake of the entertainment and the delightful stimulus to their minds which such pretence can bring. They know perfectly well that the 'Theseus' who speaks is not the real Theseus, but at the same time they know that pretending to believe in him is a necessary part of the business of coming to see and enjoy a stage play.

At any rate this is so if the audience are accustomed to attending plays, and so understand the nature of dramatic convention. A child at his first play, or an audience of rustics who had never encountered play-acting before, might be deluded into taking the image for the reality. Such a reaction would seem comic to more sophisticated play-goers; they would probably laugh at the simplicity of those who took Theseus for a real duke, Oberon for a real fairy king or Puck, Peaseblossom and Cobweb as real fairies.

And it is something very like this contrast between audiences who understand the nature of dramatic illusion and those who do not which Shakespeare makes the main comic theme of Act V, Scene 1. The difference is that he contrasts the sophisticated audience of Theseus, Hippolyta and the lovers with a naïve group of actors in the shape of Bottom and the Athenian workmen – actors who, if they were an audience, would very probably mistake illusion for reality, and so when they come to put on a play for the first time in their lives expect just such a reaction from their own audience. To prevent it they laboriously explain what is self-evident to their courtly audience, that the lion is not really a lion, but Snug, the joiner. The comedy is further increased by the fact that their acting is so bad and their notions of stage-craft (representing a wall by a man with some plaster about him, and the moon by a lantern and the man in the moon's dog) so elementary that there is never the remotest possibility of deceiving their audience that these things are real. Moreover, the text of their play, 'Pyramus and Thisby', is so clumsily written and full of such crude poetic devices that to both the courtly audience on the stage and the actual audience in the theatre, before whom *A Midsummer Night's Dream* is being performed, it will seem ridiculously inadequate to the tragic story which it is supposed to express.

The performance begins with a garbled Prologue, spoken by Quince with such little understanding of punctuation that in several places he produces something which is the exact opposite of what is intended. For example, instead of saying that the actors come 'with good will to show our simple skill' (line 110), he runs this line together with the previous one, and, gasping for breath, makes a full stop after 'good will', with the result that he seems to say, '. . . we come not to offend but with good will' – that is, we fully intend to give offence! Likewise, instead of saying, 'Our true intent is all for your delight. We are not here that you should here repent you', Quince makes a stop after 'intent is', and so produces the opposite statement that 'All for your delight we are not here' (lines 114–15).

Even in its correctly punctuated form the Prologue is an ineptly written piece, as is the verse which accompanies the dumb show. This is padded out with unnecessary phrases, like 'At the which let no man wonder' (line 133) and 'if you will know' (line 135), and is prone to say the same thing twice over, but in slightly different words, as in line 140: 'Did scare away, or rather did affright'. When some strong emotional effect is desired it is effected by such a crude use of alliteration (repetition of the same sound at the beginning of successive words) that the result is more laughable than moving:

> *Whereat with blade, with bloody blameful blade,*
> *He bravely broach'd his boiling bloody breast.*

> (lines 145–6)

Similarly overdone poetic effects are typical of the speeches of Pyramus and Thisby. Pyramus' opening speech, for example, with its extravagant 'O's and its excessive repetition of 'night' and 'alack', which are meant to make night seem mysterious and threatening, immediately has the sound of high-flown farce (lines 168–70). The same applies to his personification (addressing a thing as if it were a living being) of the wall – the joke being heightened by the fact that the 'wall' is indeed a person, namely Snout. The verse of the play-within-the-play is, at this point, in quatrains (lines rhyming ABAB), but, not content with that, the over-eager poet responsible for it (Shakespeare, of course, but Shakespeare deliberately for this purpose making himself into a bad poet) piles on internal rhyme as well 'Show me thy *chink, to blink* through with *mine eyne*' (line 175). The verse later becomes rhyming couplets (lines 195–205), and then with the lion's speech the pattern changes to ABABCCDD (lines 216–23). With Pyramus' address to the moon (lines 264–7) there is more comic personification and overdone alliteration ('thy gracious, golden, glittering gleams', line 266), presented in quatrain form. Then, as Pyramus spots the blood-stained mantle, the verse-lines become much shorter, rhyming AABCCBDDEFFE (lines 268–79), and except for four lines (283–6), this remains the pattern for the remainder of the play-within-the-play. The purpose behind this change to lyrical short lines is, no doubt, to raise the emotional temperature so that the audience will respond with heightened intensity to the tragic climax, of the deaths of Pyramus and Thisby. However, the 'bad poet' cannot keep up this high style. He relapses into commonplace endearments like 'O dainty duck! O dear!' (line 273) and absurd repetitions such as 'Now die, die, die, die, die' (line 298); and in Thisby's speech on finding Pyramus' dead body his attempts at beautiful comparisons not only produce the ridiculous let-down of 'His eyes were green as leeks' (line 326), but also lead to

verbal confusion which is reminiscent of Bottom's 'the ear of man hath
not seen . . .' at the end of Act IV, Scene 1:

> *These lily lips,*
> *This cherry nose,*
> *These yellow cowslip cheeks.*

The play of 'Pyramus and Thisby' and its actors are well matched.
Sometimes it is difficult to tell whether bad poet or bad actors are to
blame. For example, when Pyramus and Thisby swear love to each
other they compare themselves, as is so often done in Elizabethan
love poetry, with lovers whose names are famous in 'antique fable',
but either they or the author get the names muddled. For Leander and
Hero they say 'Limander' and 'Helen' (lines 195–6), confusing Hero,
for whose love Leander swam the Hellespont, with Helen, the wife of
Menelaus, who was carried off to Troy by Paris (also known as
Alexander, and hence, perhaps, the running together of Leander and
Alexander as 'Limander'). Likewise Cephalus and Procris become
'Shafalus' and 'Procrus' (lines 197–8). Flute's bad acting is certainly
responsible for the ridiculous mispronunciation of 'Ninus' tomb' (line
255) as 'Ninny's tomb' (Quince had tried to correct this mistake
during rehearsal, III.1.86–7), and Bottom's naïve eagerness to
please is responsible for the interruption (line 182) and his jumping up
immediately after Thisby dies, which shatter any dramatic illusion that
such an absurd performance might possibly have created.

All the time, however, the actual theatre audience are enjoying both
the ridiculous spectacle of the workmen's 'Pyramus and Thisby' *and*
the illusion which is being created by *A Midsummer Night's Dream,*
the highly skilful play within which 'this palpable gross play' (line 355)
is contained. The whole scene, indeed, may be regarded as a highly
entertaining exercise which contrasts true and false dramatic illusion,
the one standing out more sharply against the background of the other.

The common-sense rationality of the daytime world of Theseus and
Athens, as opposed to Oberon and the wood, also emphasises the
absurdities of 'Pyramus and Thisby', which as a love-story involving
death brought about by mistake (Pyramus is deceived by the blood-
stained mantle) might be regarded as another version of the love-
induced mistakes presented in the night-time woodland scenes. If so,
it is such mistakes seen by unflattering daylight rather than the soft,
deceptive light of the moon, confirming the general movement of the
play from day to night and back to day. However, by the time 'Pyramus
and Thisby' has been finished darkness has fallen once more, and the
witching hour of midnight has come: 'The iron tongue of midnight
hath told twelve', as Theseus says, and ''tis almost fairy time' (lines

352–3). The lovers depart to bed, and, in fact, the play ends with Puck, Oberon and Titania holding the stage, with a final return to night and the supernatural, fairy world.

Puck sets the tone for this with his speech (lines 360–79) which calls up a host of impressions contrary to daytime sanity: the roaring of the hungry lion, the wolf howling against the moon (while the day-labouring ploughman sleeps), the screeching of the owl, which is associated with death, the opening of graves (which traditionally happens at midnight) to let ghosts come out into the churchyard, and, as a climax to them all, the running of the fairies by the side of ·Hecate's horses as they draw the goddess's chariot away from the sun. Hecate is called 'triple' because she is known in heaven as Luna or Cynthia, goddess of the moon and childbirth; on earth as Diana, goddess of chastity and the hunt; and in hell as Hecate, goddess of the night. It is her night-time significance that Puck chiefly evokes in this speech, but the other associations enhance that significance, giving a sense of strange, supernatural powerfulness which profoundly disturbs the daytime assumptions that life is clear and straightforward. The very title of the play itself, *A Midsummer Night's Dream*, seems to be caught up in these associations when Puck speaks of the fairies' 'Following darkness like a dream' (line 375). And yet the evil, harmful associations are warded off: the fairies are playful ('frolic', line 376); nothing is to disturb this 'hallowed' palace of Theseus; and it is even something of an anti-climax that Puck ends by saying that he has been 'sent with broom before,/To sweep the dust behind the door' (lines 378–9).

The sacred powers of night are, then, to be put to good use. This is confirmed when Oberon, Titania and the fairies enter, hopping 'as light as bird from brier' (line 383), to sing and dance, and Oberon gives his blessing to the marriage-beds of Theseus and Hippolyta and the lovers.

Finally, Puck speaks alone once more, and in his Epilogue to the theatre audience gives yet another twist to the theme of night and dream. Himself and all the other actors who have appeared on the stage are referred to as 'shadows' (line 412) who have peopled what the audience are invited to regard as 'a dream' (line 417) through which they have slept for the last two or three hours. Most of the original Elizabethan audience would have been standing in the broad daylight of the afternoon in a theatre open to the sky, but because of the way in which Shakespeare's poetry has worked on them they have in an imaginative sense been sleeping and dreaming, allowing strange, night-time images to float up from the depths of their minds, and old 'fables' and superstitions to take over from their more usual, practical, common-sense view of life. Puck hopes, however, that the experience has been a pleasant one for them, and, as an actor who earns his living from creating such pleasant illusions, he knows that in the end his power to work on their imagination has to yield before *their* power to show pleasure or displeasure in the performance by clapping or not clapping. If this play has not seemed good to them, he hopes to make amends by presenting a better one soon. But this way of speaking is only a sort of modesty designed to win a good opinion, as boasting would not. 'Give me your hands, if we be friends' is an invitation to shake hands as friendly people do, and it is also an invitation to applaud, which the actor may confidently expect to be accepted, if he and his company have made the most of the opportunities which Shakespeare has given them.

NOTES AND GLOSSARY:

brow of Egypt: gypsy forehead

masques: an entertainment blending drama, dance and music which was particularly favoured by the Court. Some of the actors would be professionals, others courtiers

brief: résumé, short list

Centaurs: mythical creatures, half man, half horse

The riot . . . in their rage: the 'Thracian singer' was the poet and musician, Orpheus. He was torn to pieces by the female followers (the 'Bacchanals') of Bacchus, the god of wine

The thrice three Muses: the nine goddesses of the arts (Calliope = epic; Melpomene = tragedy; Thalia = comedy; Erato = love poetry; Polyhymnia = sacred poetry; Euterpe = music and lyric poetry; Clio = history; Urania = astronomy; Terpsichore = dancing)

unbreathed: unaccustomed, lacking exercise

periods: full stops

This fellow doth not stand upon points: pun – he is not over particular, and he ignores punctuation marks

stop: another pun, following up line 118. 'Stop' is a term in horse-riding for pulling up a horse, and also the full-stop in punctuation

in government: properly controlled

Jove: Jove, or Jupiter (Latin equivalent of Greek Zeus) was the chief of the gods

Limander, Helen, Shafalus, Procrus: see page 46

He should have worn the horns on his head: a stock Elizabethan joke about cuckoldry. A man whose wife had deceived him was supposed to sprout horns on his head

in snuff: a pun: to be 'in snuff' is to take offence, and when a candle-flame is put out it is 'snuffed'

Cut thread and thrum: 'Thrum' is the end of a weaver's thread, the useless bit. Thus 'cut thread and thrum' means to destroy good and bad together

pap: breast

die, ace, ass: 'Die' also means 'dice'; 'ace' = 1 on a dice; 'ass' sounds somewhat like 'ace' (and may have been nearer in sound in Elizabethan English) – hence a series of rather strained puns

Sisters Three: the three goddesses of fate (Clotho, Lachesis, Atropos) on whom man's life depends

Bergomask: a crude, rustic dance (from Bergamo, Italy)

Hecate: see page 47

Gentles: Ladies and Gentlemen

Part 3

Commentary

Love as a theme in Shakespearean comedy

Like most of Shakespeare's comedies *A Midsummer Night's Dream* is concerned with love, and like most of the comedies it is somewhat ambiguous on the subject. There is no one single approach to love, or definition of its nature, which might be said to be typical of the play. Instead, there are conflicting attitudes and assumptions which are balanced one against another.

To begin with, the play seems to offer in the situation of Hermia and Lysander, a fairly straightforward example of that division between Youth and Age which is a recurrent theme of literature and is celebrated in many an Elizabethan poem. A typical example is the opposition, in Spenser's *The Shepherd's Calendar* for 'February', between the young shepherd Cuddie, who wishes to 'carol of love' and sing hymns of praise to his 'lass's glove', and Thenot, the old shepherd, who tells him that he is a fool to boast of his love, for 'All that is lent to love will be lost'. In *A Midsummer Night's Dream* it is Egeus who plays the part of Age by insisting not only on his right as a father to choose whom his daughter shall marry, but also by treating Hermia's resistance to his will as the result of Lysander's calculated playing on the inexperience of her youth:

> *Thou, thou, Lysander, thou hast given her rhymes,*
> *And interchang'd love-tokens with my child;*
> *Thou hast by moonlight at her window sung,*
> *With feigning voice, verses of feigning love,*
> *And stol'n the impression of her fantasy*
> *With bracelets of thy hair, rings, gawds, conceits,*
> *Knacks, trifles, nosegays, sweetmeats – messengers*
> *Of strong prevailment in unhardened youth.*

(I.1.28–35)

Many of the things he mentions are the stock-in-trade of Elizabethan love poetry. The serenade by moonlight is the traditional way of wooing a mistress, and the writing of love-poems, exchanging of locks of hair and giving of small, sentimental presents are still part of the ritual of courtship today. Egeus, however, regards them as part of an elaborate pretence of love (he expresses his disbelief in Lysander's sincerity by the repetition of *'feigning* voice' and *'feigning* love'), and he dismisses them with the same contempt as that later Shakespearean father, Polonius, dismisses the 'holy vows' of Hamlet to Ophelia, which are, says Polonius, merely 'springes to catch woodcocks', that is traps for foolish birds (*Hamlet,* I.3.115).

Theseus – not so old as Egeus (he is himself about to be married), but neither so young as Hermia and Lysander – seems to support the view of Age. As his later behaviour shows, this is not quite the case, however. What he does is to act as the upholder of the law – a law perhaps made by old men. He has some sympathy with Youth, but must carry out the duties that go with his position. But neither authority nor the law can make Youth 'look' with the eyes of Age. Youth must see things its own way, and exercise free choice. Accordingly, Hermia would rather become a nun, or even die, than give herself to him 'whose unwished yoke/My soul consents not to give sovereignty' (I.1.81–2). Both she and Lysander, lamenting that it is the fate of young lovers ever to find themselves crossed in love, vehemently agree that it is hell 'to choose love by another's eyes' (I.1.140); and it is their situation, rather than the authoritarianism of Egeus, which commands the audience's sympathy. The Elizabethan respect for order, as has been pointed out, would perhaps modify this sympathy to a greater extent than is the case with a modern audience, but the balance would still tip in Hermia and Lysander's favour, partly because of the severity of the law with which they find themselves at odds and partly because of the arbitrary manner in which Egeus asserts his rights. Theirs is the romantic, but also profoundly human, appeal of Youth and freedom in conflict with the restrictions and compulsions associated with Age.

This is not the whole story, however, as the presentation of the love affair of Pyramus and Thisby shows. They, too, are thwarted by parents. In Golding's translation of Ovid's *Metamorphoses* the text reads:

> And if that right had taken place they had bene man and wife,
> But still their Parents went about to let [= prevent] which for their life
> They could not let. For both their heartes with equall flame did burne.

Love, in other words, cannot be prevented. It will find a way (as happens ultimately with Hermia and Lysander). But the way that Pyramus and Thisby find leads to disaster – a disaster which is taken seriously enough by Ovid, but which in Golding sounds unintentionally silly, and which in the play-within-the-play of *A Midsummer Night's*

Dream is made by Shakespeare deliberately ridiculous. One effect of this is to give Youth's insistence on looking with its own eyes a quite different dimension. The freedom of love becomes self-deception, and the subject for uproarious farce. The lovers' plan for a secret meeting leads to Pyramus' misinterpretation of the blood-stained mantle, and so to his suicide and Thisby's. He is deceived by appearances; the tragedy is all a mistake; and the version of it presented by the Athenian workmen, who are themselves ludicrously anxious lest the audience be deceived by appearances, throws the whole business of illusion into the greatest possible relief. The result is that a celebrated tale of youthful, romantic love is turned into an anti-romantic burlesque.

Love's folly is, in fact, as much the theme of *A Midsummer Night's Dream* as love's freedom; and in this respect 'Pyramus and Thisby' only makes more obvious something which is there from the first scene. Hermia wishes 'I would my father look'd but with my eyes' (I.1.56), and she and Lysander agree that it is hell 'to choose love by another's eyes' (line 140); but Helena takes the opposite view. 'Love looks not with the eyes, but with the mind', she says, and points to the blindness of the traditional figure of Cupid. In her view love is a 'child', or like a 'waggish boy', poor in judgement, and full of oaths that may be sworn one minute and forsworn the next. It is, in fact, the very embodiment of immaturity and instability.

Helena, moreover, speaks from experience, 'for', as she says,

ere Demetrius look'd on Hermia's eyne,
He hail'd down oaths that he was only mine.

(lines 241–2)

This experience is echoed elsewhere in the play, notably by Theseus in his speech at the beginning of Act V, and by Bottom when Titania makes her ultra-romantic declaration that his fair person compels her 'On the first view, to say, to swear, I love thee'. (In *As You Like It* Shakespeare was to emphasise the importance of love at first sight in the code of romantic love by quoting from Marlowe's love-poem, *Hero and Leander,* the line, 'Whoever loved that loved not at first sight'). Bottom's eminently sensible reply is:

Methinks, mistress, you should have little reason for that. And yet, to say the truth, reason and love keep little company together now-a-days. The more pity that some honest neighbours will not make them friends.

The failure of reason and love to keep company together is confirmed by the lovers' actual experience in the woods outside Athens.

Lysander and Demetrius chop and change their loves, not by reason, but by the capricious influence of love, symbolised by the love-juice squeezed from the appropriately named flower, 'love-in-idleness'. The fact that Lysander specifically claims to have transferred his love from Hermia to Helena because 'The will of man is by his reason sway'd', and says that reason has now become 'the marshal' to his 'will' (II.2.115–20), only serves to make love's irrationality more obvious. This is matched in its absurdity by the extravagant words of praise ('O Helen, goddess, nymph, perfect, divine', III.2.137) which Demetrius, having previously told Helena that he is sick when he looks on her, addresses to her when he wakes under the influence of the love-juice. Although Demetrius claims that his heart was only Hermia's 'guest' and is now returned to its 'home' in Helena (171–2), there is as little reason in his change as in Lysander's. Likewise, Hermia and Helena's desertion of their long and intimate friendship, to quarrel in petty and spiteful terms, shows them to be equally inconsistent and irrational. Add to this that Oberon and Titania, though they are on one level exotic and mysterious super-natural beings, also behave in their quarrel like ordinary jealous human beings, and that hints are given that even the solid and sensible Theseus has been involved in dubious adventures with Perigouna, Aegles, Ariadne and Antiopa (II.2.77–80), and it is apparent that the representation of romance and the romantic adventures of young love is balanced by an awareness of its irrationality and absurdity which is just as strongly *anti*-romantic.

The romantic in *A Midsummer Night's Dream* is balanced, then, by the anti-romantic, but not destroyed by it. They complement each other. This is seen in the very structure of the play, which, as already indicated, moves from light to darkness and back to light again; but, as if to prevent the simple conclusion that the disturbances of the night are over and can be forgotten, the play ends with the re-appearance of the fairies. They, too, however, represent a compromise with daylight in that they come to bless, not to curse, the issue of the marriages which have just been celebrated.

Development of the plot

In the development of the plot situations are created which are potentially tragic. The play opens with such a situation, threatening disorder within the family as Egeus insists on his right to dispose of his daughter in marriage as he pleases, and Hermia asserts her preference for Lysander, even though it may bring upon her the full severity of the Athenian law. The lovers are brought into conflict with each other, to the point where Helena has to run away to escape the fury of Hermia, and Lysander and Demetrius draw their swords to fight a duel. The quarrel of Oberon and Titania brings in its train a 'progeny of evils', described in a speech (II.1.81–117) which might be compared with Burgundy's description in *Henry V* (V.2.29–67) of the ravages wrought by war on 'this best garden of the world,/Our fertile France'. But at the same time the audience have the sense that these destructive potentialities are contained within bounds. The quarrel of the lovers, for example, is never allowed to get out of hand. Lysander and Demetrius are led up and down by Puck so that their threats cannot be put into practice, and Oberon is always near at hand to ensure that the mistakes of the night – sometimes wantonly pursued by Puck – will not pass the bounds from comedy to tragedy. Oberon expresses his annoyance with Titania by making her fall in love with the transformed Bottom, and that most uproariously comic scene becomes a safety valve for dangerous emotions. It has the same farcical nature as the later play-within-a-play of Pyramus and Thisby, the subject of which is tragedy, but which diverts anxiety and distress into ridicule and laughter. Lastly, the events of the night, which have been directed towards pairing off Demetrius with Helena and restoring Lysander to Hermia, leave Egeus with no alternative but to accept Lysander as his son-in-law, and all is settled amicably.

This drive towards a happy ending is in interesting contrast with the end of *Love's Labour's Lost,* the comedy which immediately preceded *A Midsummer Night's Dream.* In *Love's Labour's Lost* the follies of love were emphasised so as to bring to their senses some rather foolish male lovers (the women were exempted), but the play concluded, not with marriage, but with a period of probation in which the lovers were to prove themselves as seriously worthy of their future wives. As one of them, Berowne, is made to say,

> *Our wooing doth not end like an old play:*
> *Jack hath not Jill.*
>
> > (*Love's Labour's Lost,* V.2.862–3)

There is a deliberate reference to this at the end of *A Midsummer Night's Dream,* Act III, when Puck, using the love-juice to make Lysander fall in love with Hermia again, says:

> *Jack shall have Jill;*
> *Nought shall go ill;*
> *The man shall have this mare again, and all shall be well.*
>
> > (III.2.461–3)

Comedy by definition has a happy ending. *Love's Labour's Lost,* as its title suggests, is a not-quite-comedy; but *A Midsummer Night's Dream* finds the complete 'concord' of its 'discord' and so qualifies as a full comedy.

Why, then, the 'discord' in the first place? Partly because the business of drama, in whatever form, is to imitate life – as Hamlet says, 'to hold, as 'twere, the mirror up to nature; to show virtue her own feature, scorn her own image, and the very age and body of the time his form and pressure' (*Hamlet*, III.2.23–7). This would not be done if life were represented as free from conflict and distress. Another reason is that the happy ending which issues out of tribulation and threats of disaster is felt to be that much sweeter. But the main reason must be that comedy, like a painting, offers the pleasures of contrast and balance, one mass setting off another, colours clashing as well as blending, light standing out against the shade. When acted in the theatre (and one must always remember that Shakespeare wrote a script for performance rather than a book to be read) *A Midsummer Night's Dream* is full of visual contrasts: the splendidly regal Theseus and Hippolyta, with all the trappings of their court, and the coarsely dressed Athenian workmen; the delicacy and swiftly flitting movements of Titania and her attendant fairies, and the gross vulgarity of Bottom with the ass's head; Lysander and Demetrius, swords drawn, but bewildered by Puck, and the entry of Theseus and his hunters. Far more important, however, are the contrasts of character, mood and language. It is through these that the special tone and atmosphere of the play are created, that mingled dye which is the peculiar poetic quality of *A Midsummer Night's Dream*.

The characters

Bottom

Although Shakespeare is a great creator of characters – one thinks of Falstaff, Hamlet, Cleopatra, Caliban – this particular play lacks characterisation of profound psychological penetration. Probably the most memorable character is Bottom, and he is not fascinating by virtue of the complexity or richness of his personality. Like all the Athenian workmen he is slightly dull, honest, literal-minded and naïve, eager to please, but ill-equipped to understand the nature of the dramatic illusion by which he hopes to please a sophisticated audience. To Puck he is 'the shallowest thickskin of that barren sort' (III.2.13), but, in fact, there is little evidence to suggest that he is less intelligent than the rest. On the contrary, he is always ready with solutions to their problems (however ridiculous those solutions may appear), but he is chiefly differentiated from the rest by his enthusiasm, self-confidence, assertiveness and laughable, yet unobjectionable, egotism. Without him the others are helpless, for the very brashness of his self-confidence is needed to carry them through the difficulties, real or imaginary, which seem to face them at every turn as they prepare the performance of their play. Flute speaks for them all when he says, 'If he come not, then the play is marr'd; it goes not forward, doth it?' (IV.1.5–6). From the moment Bottom appears he establishes himself as the strongest personality among the workmen, and as their natural leader, despite the fact that Quince is nominally in charge of the rehearsals. They instinctively recognise that he would be 'the man of the match', the one to be singled out by the Duke as the greatest success, if 'Pyramus and Thisby' were favoured, and likely to receive the highest reward ('he could not have scaped sixpence a day', says the boyish Flute, who seems to hero-worship Bottom). Not that Bottom is much of a team man. He is so full of energy and belief in himself that he would take all the parts in the play if he could, and turn 'Pyramus and Thisby' into a one-man show.

More striking still, however, is Bottom's capacity to adapt himself to the totally unfamiliar situation of finding himself beloved by the Queen of Fairies. He knows that Titania's behaviour is irrational and that he is neither 'wise' nor 'beautiful' (III.1.135), and perhaps he knows that he is, in effect, a prisoner (certainly Titania tells him so: 'Thou shalt remain here whether thou wilt or no', line 139), but none of this discomposes him. Titania calls him a 'gentleman' (line 150), which the Elizabethans would immediately see as ridiculous, but it is precisely as one of nature's gentlemen that he behaves towards her attendant fairies. It may well have been a further joke to the Elizabethans that he calls fairies – and servant fairies at that – 'your worship' and 'honest gentleman' (lines 166 and 170), but his courtesy is most attractive. The gulf between him and them is huge (that he is placed in such a situation *vis à vis* them is part of the pattern of contrasts which makes up this play), and is emphasised by Titania's promise to 'purge' his 'mortal grossness' so that he will 'like an airy spirit go' (lines 146–7). Yet his capacity to bridge that gulf with such ease is the more remarkable thing.

Bottom goes on to show even greater resilience when he is restored to his normal shape. It seems to him that he has had 'a most rare vision' (IV.1.203), and, though stumbling into a characteristic linguistic absurdity with his 'eye of man hath not heard', etc., the confused biblical quotation still manages to communicate his sense of wonder and ecstasy. Moreover, he quickly plans to turn it to good use by having Peter Quince write a ballad of it, to be called 'Bottom's Dream', which will be sung at Thisby's death. (In Act V, however, this seems to have been forgotten.) The combination of rapture, practicality, self-confidence and egotism is typical of the man. At this moment he seems the very centre of the play: *A Midsummer Night's Dream* is, at least momentarily, 'Bottom's Dream'. He holds the stage alone, and the audience are captivated. They laugh *at* him, but they also laugh *with* him, finding him both a figure of fun and a figure of triumphant adaptability, as much at home among the fairies as among his Athenian workmates.

Puck

Theseus and Puck also enjoy something of this pivotal position in *A Midsummer Night's Dream*, though with never the hold on the audience's sympathies that Bottom gains. Puck moves in the world of fairy and also in the world of human beings, playing the boyish pranks described by himself and one of the fairies at the beginning of Act II. As Oberon's not altogether reliable lieutenant he also intervenes in the action of the play to add confusion to the lovers and the workmen alike. He positively delights in mischief. The distresses of the lovers, which his own mistake has increased, are to him simply a 'fond [foolish] pageant', and his comment is the detached 'Lord, what fools these mortals be!' (III.2.114–15). The crosses of love are 'sport', and he gleefully admits that

> *those things do best please me*
> *That befall prepost'rously.*

(lines 120–1)

When he joins in, it is not to become emotionally involved, but to stir up more material for mocking laughter. That the audience nevertheless find him likeable and entertaining is due to their instinctive recognition that human standards do not apply to him – and to the fact that he embodies that love of practical jokes which is present in everyone, but which can be expressed by Puck with an uncomplicated zest impossible to human beings who must inevitably feel, 'There but for the grace of God go I'. This very detachment, however, gives him uncertain status in the audience's eyes. They cannot share his laughter to the full, because it is the laughter of a being immune from human feeling.

Theseus

Theseus is often judged by his speech at the beginning of Act V, where he appears as the sceptic, inclined to play down the extravagances of imagination and judge reality in the light of 'cool reason'. But not only does this ignore the far more positive way in which the workings of the poetic imagination are described, it also fails to take into account his later remarks on the need for generosity in responding to the offerings of subjects whose goodwill exceeds their ability:

> *what poor duty cannot do, noble respect*
> *Takes it in might, not merit.*
>
> (V.1.91–2)

His character seems to be that of a humane country gentleman (witness his enthusiasm for his hounds at IV.1.116–23), grafted on to that of a duty-conscious head of state, as shown in the way he upholds the Athenian law in the first scene, and with touches of a romantic lover eager for the consummation of his marriage and, as suggested by Oberon, of a man with a philandering past. These elements do not add up to a very clear or consistent character. Probably what concerned Shakespeare more was the dramatic function which Theseus had to serve at different points in the play. Thus, at the beginning his rôle as upholder of the law is paramount because of the needs of the Egeus – Hermia situation. After the lovers' adventures in the woods, the return to Athens, daylight and reason calls for a strong spokesman for those values. As this spokesman Theseus makes a contrast with what has gone before, and, of course, he also contrasts with Hippolyta who is more inclined to believe what the lovers say. A few lines later they change rôles, Hippolyta doubting the worth of the workmen's offering, Theseus defending it. An actor can accommodate these changes quite comfortably, and since the emphasis is on contrasting views the slight inconsistency in characterisation which seems to be involved is unimportant.

Oberon

If there is a ruler whose power and influence are really felt in *A Midsummer Night's Dream*, it is Oberon. He is an imperious and peremptory figure. His very first words are both sharp and authoritative: 'Ill met by moonlight, proud Titania' (II.1.60). Titania retorts with 'jealous Oberon!', and jealous he is in the sense that he wants Titania's Indian boy, though precisely why is not made clear. It is enough that it is his will, which he is not prepared to have thwarted. He is a dark, elemental force; not vicious, or aloof from human sympathy, for it is he who takes pity on Helena even while he is pursuing his vengeance on Titania, but arbitrary – to that extent like a haughty god – unaccustomed to having his wishes debated, and strong in the knowledge that what he wants he has the power to exact. And that power is mysteriously supernatural. He can see, as even Puck cannot, Cupid flying 'between the cold moon and the earth' (II.1.156), and be a companion to Aurora, goddess of the dawn (III.2.389). He also knows the force of herbs, like a witch, but without a witch's evil malignancy, and he can cast a spell on a new-born child, but one that *protects* the child from harm (V.1.398–403). Above all, his nature is expressed in the poetry he speaks:

> *Thou rememb'rest*
> *Since once I sat upon a promontory,*
> *And heard a mermaid on a dolphin's back*
> *Uttering such dulcet and harmonious breath*
> *That the rude sea grew civil at her song,*
> *And certain stars shot madly from their spheres*
> *To hear the sea-maid's music.*
>
> (II.1.148–54)

These lines describe the effect of the mermaid's song rather than inform one about Oberon's character, but it is the fact that Oberon can perceive such things, that he inhabits a realm where such things happen, that tells one most about his nature. This realm is as far from the rational, common-sense world for which Theseus is the spokesman at the beginning of Act V as it is possible to be, and only the language of the play can carry the audience there. It is a dream world, essentially imaginative and profoundly irrational, with the illogicality and unpredictability of dreams. What it tells about Oberon is that he, too, is a dream figure, powerful in his influence on the human world, but not to be tied to its laws.

Titania

Much the same requires to be said of Titania. She, too, is 'proud', and not easily to be mastered by her consort. To his 'Tarry, rash wanton; am not I thy lord?' she replies, 'Then I must be thy lady' (II.1.63–4). And she, too, expresses her character most of all in the poetry she speaks, but that character is more sensuous and physical than his. It is evoked, for example, in the speech which describes the consequences of their quarrel (lines 81–117) and especially in her account of her friendship with the mother of the Indian boy, which balances the sense of devastation in the previous speech with an overwhelming sense of richness and fertility (lines 123–34).

Hermia, Helena, Lysander and Demetrius

After such beings the lovers, Hermia, Helena, Lysander and Demetrius, seem pale and uninteresting figures. As persons they have little individual existence. Helena is distinguished from Hermia by her greater height, which is also accompanied by greater timidity, but these are such superficial differences that it almost seems that they are introduced to save the audience from confusing the two heroines. The heroes are not distinguished even to that degree; which is oddly appropriate since they behave exactly like each other in switching their allegiances. But, again, for the purposes of this play such weakness of characterisation matters very little. They are the young lovers of romance literature, and they speak the love-language of the Elizabethan sonnet (except when quarrelling, when they comically come down to a more vulgar level). It is the theme of young love rather than the fortunes of four particularised young lovers with which the play is concerned, and for the expression of that theme these characterless characters will do.

Atmosphere and imagery

In atmosphere *A Midsummer Night's Dream* is a blend of the artificial and the natural. The revived interest in antiquity which in so much Elizabethan literature leads to frequent references to the gods and goddesses, and the places and persons of classical mythology, is to be found here, too. Theseus and Hippolyta derive from this 'antique' world, as do Pyramus and Thisby and the names of the lovers, especially Lysander. Among other classical references are the following: Cupid and Venus (to be expected in a love comedy of this kind); Diana, the goddess of chastity (see I.1.88 and IV.1.109); Apollo, god of the sun and poetry, who pursued the nymph, Daphne (II.1.231); Neptune, god of the sea (I.1.126 and III.2.92), and Aurora, goddess of the dawn (III:2.380); Aeneas, the Trojan warrior who founded Rome, and his love for Dido, Queen of Carthage (I.1.173–4); Theseus' previous love-affairs (II.1.78 *et seq.*) and his kinship with Hercules and Cadmus; and places in Greece such as Crete, Sparta and Thessaly (besides the setting of the play in Athens). The rejected wedding entertainments in Act V also include references to the battle of the Centaurs (mythical creatures who were half horses, half men) and to the Bacchanalia in which Orpheus was torn to pieces. All these heighten the sense of being in a strange world which is imaginatively exciting because exotic and remote.

Classical references, however, are far exceeded, both in number and poetic quality, by the references to a more familiarly English world of birds, beasts and flowers. This is in part accounted for by the importance of the love-juice, derived from the pansy, or 'love-in-idleness', and the transformation of Bottom by means of the ass's head, but such references are far more plentiful than the plot of *A Midsummer Night's Dream* would require. They appear in all parts of the play, but especially in connection with the fairies. They cluster thickly, for example, in Oberon's description of the bank where Titania sleeps:

> *I know a bank where the wild thyme blows,*
> *Where oxlips and the nodding violet grows,*
> *Quite over-canopied with luscious woodbine,*
> *With sweet musk-roses, and with eglantine;*
> *There sleeps Titania sometime of the night,*
> *Lull'd in these flowers with dances and delight;*
> *And there the snake throws her enamell'd skin,*
> *Weed wide enough to wrap a fairy in.*

(II.1.249–56)

The critical danger is to regard a passage of this kind as merely pretty decoration. It is, in fact, essential to the creation of a fairy world which is exotic and voluptuous (notice the effect of saturation in 'over-canopied with *luscious* woodbine'), but also vividly real and closely linked to that natural, rural experience which, despite the growth of London, still remained the common possession of Elizabethans. The discarded skin of the snake as a 'weed' (a garment) big enough for a fairy has at once the imaginative appeal of strangeness and the immediate impact of recognition – it is something concrete and known which can be used to make a strange, supernatural being come alive for the audience. It is a precise, miniature example of the ability of 'the poet's pen', as Theseus says, to give 'to airy nothing/A local habitation and a name'.

The range of natural reference is astonishing. To the flowers mentioned in Oberon's speech can be added the rose whose lap is filled with 'hoary-headed frosts' in Titania's 'forgeries of jealousy' speech (II.1.108); the musk-roses which she sticks in Bottom's 'sleek smooth head' (IV.1.3); the woodbine weaving itself into the honeysuckle and the ivy circling the elm, which she uses as images for her own embracing of Bottom; and the cowslips which are beautifully personified by the fairy in Act II, Scene 1:

> *The cowslips tall her pensioners be;*
> *In their gold coats spots you see;*
> *Those be rubies, fairy favours,*
> *In those freckles live their savours.*
> *I must go seek some dewdrops here,*
> *And hang a pearl in every cowslip's ear.*

(lines 10–15)

The lusciousness of Titania's fairy world is extended by the inclusion of fruits and berries such as 'apricocks and dewberries', 'purple grapes, green figs, and mulberries' (where native and foreign are mixed) and honey still carried in the bees' honey-bags (III.1.152–4). Its rarity and delicacy are suggested by the use of bees' 'waxen thighs' as tapers, to be lit at 'fiery glow-worm's eyes', and the use of 'the wings of painted butterflies' as fans (lines 155–9). Its enemies are 'thorny hedgehogs', 'newts', 'blind-worms' (slow-worms, legless lizards with minute eyes), 'spiders', 'beetles black', 'worm' (snake) and 'snail' – some of which are, in reality, innocuous, but were thought to be harmful, and as creeping, crawling things are the antithesis to Titania's nimble, airy followers.

Oberon, appropriately to his different character, as well as to the needs of the plot, evokes fiercer, more terrifying or disgusting creatures: 'lion', 'bear', 'wolf', 'bull', 'monkey', 'ape' (II.1.180–1) 'ounce' (lynx), 'cat' (probably lion or tiger), 'pard' (leopard) and 'boar' (II.2.30–1). Puck makes fun of 'a fat and bean-fed horse' which is sexually excited and tantalised by his imitation of the neighing of a female foal (II.1.45–6), and when he teases the Athenian workmen it is by adopting the elusive forms of horse, hound, hog or headless bear (III.1.99–101).

All these are images and references which link the natural world with the fairies, but it is by no means only in conjunction with the fairies that such images appear. Already Puck is seen adding to the list when he is bewildering the workmen, and it is a simple step from there to Bottom, in the same scene, singing, to keep his courage up, a song entirely about birds – appropriately of the commoner, almost domestic variety: 'the ousel cock' (male blackbird), 'throstle' (song-thrush), 'wren', 'finch', 'sparrow', 'lark' and 'cuckoo' (III.1.114–20). The tone of the references changes, too. Instead of adding poetic richness, as they mostly do when connected with the fairies (though Puck is again an exception), they introduce a comic note. An interest-ing example of this is the way the honey-bags, which, as already noted, heighten the lusciousness of Titania's world, when introduced in con-junction with Bottom and the fairies become a source of delightful humour. Thus, Bottom calls for Cobweb to bring him a honey-bag, but adds anxiously, '. . . and, good mounsier, have a care the honey-bag break not; I would be loath to have you overflowen with a honey-bag, signior' (IV.1.12–15).

In a similar manner flowers and other natural references are linked with the lovers. Theseus, for example, warns Hermia of the un-pleasantness of perpetual maidenhood in terms of 'the rose distill'd' as compared with that which withers 'on the virgin thorn' (I.1.76–7); Hermia tells Helena that she is to meet Lysander 'in the wood where often you and I/Upon faint primrose beds were wont to lie' (I.1.214–15); and Helena praises Hermia's voice in pastoral terms:

> *and your tongue's sweet air*
> *More tuneable than lark to shepherd's ear,*
> *When wheat is green, when hawthorn buds appear.*
>
> (I.1.183–5)

These, too, modulate into the comic elsewhere. Demetrius, awaking and turning immediately from contempt to adoration of Helena, looks for comparisons to express her superlative beauty and finds them in nature:

> *O, how ripe in show*
> *Thy lips, those kissing cherries, tempting grow!*
> *That pure congealed white, high Taurus' snow,*
> *Fann'd with the eastern wind, turns to a crow*
> *When thou hold'st up thy hand.*
>
> (III.2.139–42)

And, more ludicrous still, in the rehearsal of 'Pyramus and Thisby' Bottom, attempting a romantic comparison of Thisby's breath to the scent of flowers, stumbles on flowers of 'odious (instead of "odorous") savours sweet', thus converting her breath to a hateful smell.

On the other hand, the serpent which Hermia dreams of shortly before discovering that Lysander has deserted her (II.2.145–50) is more serious in tone than, for example, the 'spotted snakes with double tongue' which are to be banished from the presence of the fairy queen (II.2.9). The cross-connection works in this case to deepen the emotional force of the lovers' plot rather than to throw into relief its comic aspects. But whichever way it works, it helps to strengthen the sense of interrelation between the different worlds of the play – those of the fairies, the lovers, the workmen and of Theseus – and to create an impression that there exists a larger, more complete, poetic world in which these otherwise separate worlds are joined together. Joined, but not, of course, made identical. They retain their separate characteristics, and much of the enjoyment of the play derives from the contrasts and contradictions which their separateness makes possible; but over and above that there is a larger imaginative unity, created through the parallels of plot and these cross-connecting images and references, which helps to make *A Midsummer Night's Dream* one harmonious whole.

In a single phrase – if it is not too foolish to attempt to sum up so rich a comedy as *A Midsummer Night's Dream* in a single phrase –

the chief characteristic of this play is unity in diversity. It is a very Elizabethan quality. It is what Elizabethan architects, for example, attempted to achieve in their formal and yet fussily elaborate halls and houses, and it is what Spenser intended to create in *The Faerie Queene,* where he combined extraordinarily complex, interweaving stories involving hundreds of characters with a bold, basic design in which each book of his poem would be presided over by one knight representing one of the twelve moral virtues described by Aristotle. Shakespeare could not, of course, complicate matters to that extent in a play intended for public performance in the space of two hours or so, but he could nonetheless suggest through his contrasting characters and events and wide range of reference, which were at the same time linked and cross-connected, this highly desirable Elizabethan quality of unity in diversity. So much is this an almost instinctive purpose in *A Midsummer Night's Dream* that it enters every nook and cranny, and expresses itself in the very style of the play.

Metrical structures in the play

The basic metrical line here, as in the rest of Shakespeare's plays, and in Elizabethan drama generally, is the unrhymed iambic pentameter, or 'blank verse' line. This is a line of ten syllables which may be divided into five units, or 'feet', each of which consists of an iamb, i.e. an unstressed syllable (˘) followed by a stressed syllable (´), thus:

The séal/ĭng-dáy/bĕtwíxt/my lóve/ănd mé.

(I.1.84)

However, few lines actually conform to the basic metre as closely as this. The first two lines of the play, for example, perhaps scan as follows (one says 'perhaps' because absolute accuracy is impossible in English scansion):

Nów,/fáir Híp/pólў̆tă,/oŭr núp/tĭal hóur
Dráws oň/ăpaće;/fóur háp/pў̆ days/brĭng ĭn.

The change to a stressed syllable followed by an unstressed syllable (´ ˘), instead of the 'normal' unstressed/stressed (˘ ´), at the beginning of the second line is a very common variation, but the sequences of two stressed syllables at the beginning of the first line ('Nów, fáir') and in the middle of the second ('fóur háppy') are rather more unusual. These can be explained as there for a special purpose: 'Nów, fáir . . .', involving as it does a slight pause after 'Now', opens the play with a flourish; and 'fóur háppў̆' (instead of 'fŏur háppy') gives 'four' a little extra emphasis so that the number is driven home. (Theseus goes on to complain how slowly the time seems to pass, but Hippolyta, picking up this emphasis on 'four', says,

Fóur dáys will quickly steep themselves in night;
Fóur níghts will quickly dream away the time.)

But one should not always look for this sort of explanation. A succession of perfectly regular iambic pentameters would produce a very boringly sing-song kind of verse – the mark of a bad poet, in fact. Shakespeare's skill is shown in the natural-seeming rhythm of his verse, which is the result, not of variations which are in every instance deliberately purposive, but of an instinctive accommodation between regular metric pattern and the irregular rhythms of ordinary speech.

The iambic pentameter, then, forms the groundwork of the verse in *A Midsummer Night's Dream,* but most individual lines depart from it to some extent, so that diversity is constantly being achieved within the overall unity of versification. Still more variety comes in the change from unrhymed to rhymed verse in many places and, most strikingly of all, to shorter rhymed lines which have an effect equivalent to a sudden change of rhythm and pace in a piece of music.

The first example of change from unrhymed to rhymed pentameters comes in the dialogue between Lysander and Hermia at I.1.171 and lasts for the rest of the scene. Rhyme also occurs at II.1.14–59 and 249–68; II.2.35–156 (lines 35–8 being in quatrain form, i.e. rhyming ABAB); III.1.96–101 (where the pattern is ABABCC) and 138–47, 151–60 (where each of Titania's lines ends with the same sound) and 182–6 (rhyming ABABB); III.2.5–194 (with ABABCC, DEDEFF at 122–33) and 340–447; and IV.1.1–4 (ABAB) and 82–9 (another sequence of lines ending with the same sound). This is not an exhaustive list. It excludes, for example, a number of pairs of rhymed lines (couplets) with which certain characters make their exits (II.1.144–5, 241–2, 243–4; III.2.342–3; etc.). The particular effect of these rhymed passages is variable. As explained in the scene-by-scene commentary, the switch to rhyme in the first scene heightens the romantic feeling at that point, and the sequence of similar endings at III.1.151–60 enhances the delicacy and sensuousness of Titania in contrast with Bottom. But the rhyme used in II.2 and III.2, where first Lysander and then Demetrius declare extravagant love for Helena, intensifies the artificiality of their sentiments. Always, however, the rhyme serves the general purpose of adding variety and decorativeness to the expression. This is, of course, most noticeable where rhyme alternates with prose, as it does in the Titania – Bottom section of III.1, but it applies also to such a scene as II.1, where Puck tells of his practical jokes in rhyme and is succeeded by Oberon and Titania quarrelling (more seriously) in blank verse. Titania then makes her exit with a pert couplet, to be followed by Oberon's 'love-in-idleness' speech in blank verse once more and the dialogue between the love-sick Helena and the contemptuous Demetrius, also in blank verse. This also ends with 'exit rhyme', and then the scene is rounded off with Oberon's exotic 'I know a bank where the wild thyme blows' which is rhymed throughout.

All the shorter-lined lyrical passages are rhymed. Excluding for the moment Bottom's piece of recitation in I.2, the first of these occurs at the beginning of II.1 when the Fairy whom Puck questions says:

> *Over hill, over dale,*
> *Thorough bush, thorough brier,*
> *Over park, over pale,*
> *Thorough flood, thorough fire,*
> *I do wander every where,*
> *Swifter than the moon's sphere.*

Here not only is the line shorter, and for that reason distinguished from the iambic pentameter norm, but its tripping rhythm is also markedly different. The first four lines are in rising metre (˘ ˘ / ˘ ˘ /), which immediately sounds quite different from anything that has been heard in the play before, and helps to establish the fact that we have entered the fairy world. It is, however, too strongly patterned a metre for Shakespeare to use it continuously for the fairies. As we have seen, he returns to blank verse and rhymed pentameters; but from time to time he interpolates songs which have a tripping rhythm with many unstressed syllables, such as

> *Phílŏmĕl with mélŏdў*
> *Síng ĭn oŭr swéet lúllābў.*
> *Lúllă, lúllă, lúllābў; lúllă, lúllă, lúllābў.*

(II.1.13–15)

And a special form of shorter verse, consisting of three stressed syllables in a seven-syllabled line, is used to single out certain speeches uttered by the fairies (and notably Oberon and Puck), giving them dramatic prominence. This is the verse used when Oberon squeezes the flower on Titania's eyelids (II.1.27–8) and when he speaks of the power of love-in-idleness to make a lover fall in love with the first person he sees:

> *Flówĕr ŏf thĭs púrplĕ dýe,*
> *Hít wĭth Cúpĭd's árchĕrў,*
> *Sínk ĭn ápple ŏf hĭs éye.*

(III.2.102–4)

Further, and deliberately burlesque, variation comes with the verse of the play-within-the-play. This is anticipated by Bottom's 'tyrant's vein', with its mechanical te-tum, te-tum:

> Thĕ rágĭng rócks
> Aňd shíverĭňg shócks
> Shăll bréak thĕ lócks
> Ŏf prísoň gátes, etc.

(I.2.25–8)

('Shivering' is, in this case, almost certainly pronounced 'shiv'ring'.) 'Pyramus and Thisby' is in this metre ('Bŭt stáy, Ŏ spíte!' etc.), and part of the farcical effect is to hear violence being done to the normal stresses of words to make them fit, by hook or by crook, into this mechanical pattern. Thus, at V.1.318–19, when Thisby finds Pyramus lying dead, instead of the natural 'Spéak, spéak' and 'Déad, déad?' we get:

> Spĕak, spéak. Quīte dúmb?
> Dĕad, déad? Ă tómb –

a ridiculous forcing of rhythm which, quite apart from anything else in the performance, completely empties the tragic moment of its tragedy.

Metre and rhyme in this case also point up the naïvely repetitive patterning of the words: 'Speak, speak' exactly set against 'Dead, dead'. The same naïveté is seen in the way the 'bad poet' of 'Pyramus and Thisby' uses alliteration, e.g. Pyramus' 'That liv'd, that lov'd, that lik'd, that look'd with cheer' (line 286), where living, loving, liking and looking are strung together merely because they are words beginning with 'l'. Puck can also on occasion use mechanically patterned words, but when he does so it is with the conscious purpose of making a ridiculous situation sound ridiculous. Thus, he tells the audience, at III.1.98–101, how he intends to frighten the workmen, using a deliberately artificial style:

> Sometime a horse I'll be, sometime a hound,
> A hog, a headless bear, sometime a fire;
> And neigh, and bark, and grunt, and roar, and burn,
> Like horse, hound, hog, bear, fire, at every turn.

Each noun in the last line of the quotation is exactly matched with the verb in the preceding line ('neigh' like 'horse', 'bark' like 'hound', etc.) in a way that suggests a very mechanical approach to comparisons, but Puck tosses them off so rapidly that the audience immediately appreciates that he is making fun of the whole process.

And yet there is a great deal of verbal patterning in *A Midsummer Night's Dream* which is not there merely for comic effect. We are not meant to laugh when Hermia and Lysander speak of the crosses of true love in phrases that parallel one another with as much formality as the steps of an old-fashioned dance:

> LYS. *The course of true love never did run smooth;*
> *But either it was different in blood –*
> HER. *O cross! too high to be enthrall'd to low!*
> LYS. *Or else misgraffed in respect of years –*
> HER. *O spite! too old to be engag'd to young!*
> LYS. *Or else it stood upon the choice of friends –*
> HER. *O hell! to choose love by another's eyes.*

> (I.1.134–40)

Each cross is enumerated in one line by Lysander in the form of 'either . . . or else . . . or else' and answered by Hermia with one line amplifying the nature of the cross, which is introduced by a similar exclamation: 'O cross! . . . O spite! . . . O hell!'

Later in the same scene the line-against-line pattern is used in the dialogue between Hermia and Helena in which Hermia speaks of her rejection of Demetrius' love, and Helena, taking up Hermia's words, changes them to express her own longing for Demetrius. Hermia's 'The more I hate, the more he follows me' becomes Helena's 'The more I love, the more he hateth me' (lines 198–9), and Hermia's 'His folly, Helena, is no fault of mine' is answered by Helena's 'None, but your beauty; would that fault were mine!' (lines 200–1). Such neat play upon words has a curiously ambiguous effect. It intensifies the contrast between Hermia's and Helena's situation – the very fact that the words are so similar throws into greater relief the differences which exist between them ('follows' as against 'hateth', for example, and 'fault *of* mine' as against 'fault *were* mine'); but the neatness also makes us conscious that words are being played with. It is as if the dramatist can afford the luxury of such patterning, because he knows that, despite the present stress of emotion, all is going to come right in the end. Just as the whole play is shaped towards an ultimately happy ending, and we sense, as suggested earlier, that Oberon is in control and that the reasonable Theseus is likely to come down on the side of common sense, so the very patterning of the words which express the lovers' anguish hints at an artificially controlling force which is at work to ensure that their anguish does not develop into tragic catastrophe.

Such patterning goes on right through the play. It is present, for example, in II.1.242 when Helena complains that girls cannot fight for love like men: 'We should *be woo'd*, and were not made *to woo*'. The

slight change from the passive 'be woo'd' to the active 'to woo' make us
more sharply aware of the difference between feminine waiting for
love to come and masculine searching out and active pursuit of love.
And to show that such a way of speaking is not confined to the lovers,
it can be found in use by Oberon when, at III.2.91, he rebukes Puck
for having mistaken Lysander for Demetrius with the result that what
he has brought about is 'Some true love turn'd, and not a false turn'd
true'. Here 'true' and 'turn'd' are repeated in opposite order, creating
a slightly bewildering effect (the meaning is that a true love has been
turned into a false one instead of a false love being turned into a true
one), which, however, is very appropriate to the confused situation
that has been brought about by Puck's mistake. At IV.1.68–9, when
Oberon restores Titania to her former state of mind, he again uses
verbal patterning, but of a more straightforward kind:

> *Be as thou wast wont to be;*
> *See as thou was wont to see.*

This could be expressed more compactly by some such sentence as 'Be
and see as before', but the repetition of 'be' and 'see' and the parallel
phrasing of the two lines makes everything perfectly clear and simple,
providing a verbal equivalent of the restoration of order and normality
which is now taking place in the action of the play.

The mixing of the elements

What Shakespeare seems most concerned to achieve, then, in *A
Midsummer Night's Dream* is a mixture of elements and a style which
will enable him to be serious and not too serious at the same time. Plot
is quite important and so is character, but neither is an end in itself.
Both are subordinate to a less easily definable mood and atmosphere
which is created through the interaction of plot, character and
language. To understand this atmosphere we need to examine the way
in which the play throws up both romantic and anti-romantic attitudes
to love, and yet manages to resolve their contradiction; the way in
which reason and good sense are emphasised, and yet imagination is
stimulated by fantastic contrasts and the creation of an exotic fairy
world; and the way in which the very style of the play alters to suit the
needs of passion or burlesque, whilst hinting through its artificiality
that all this is indeed a play, an entertainment rather than a realistic
representation of what life is actually like, and more particularly a
comedy which may have moments that disturb, but will find its way
past them to a happy ending and a celebration of harmony and hope for
the future.

What more than anything else seems to typify this special atmosphere of *A Midsummer Night's Dream* is the idea of 'dream' itself and the closely associated quality of moonlight. A play is a kind of dream, something which, while it lasts, feels real enough, but from which we wake to a knowledge that it was in fact unreal. At the same time the experience of the dream can be so powerful that waking from it leaves us uncertain which is truer, the dream world or the real world. A comment of this sort is made within the dream world of this play when the lovers, wakened by the horns of Theseus and his hunters, find it difficult to distinguish between the world in which they now find themselves and the bewildering world of the woodland and its magic from which they have just emerged:

> DEM. *These things seem small and undistinguishable*
> *Like far-off mountains turned into clouds.*
> HER. *Methinks I see these things with parted eye,*
> *When every thing seems double.*
> HEL. *So methinks;*
> *And I have found Demetrius like a jewel,*
> *Mine own, and not mine own.*
> DEM. *Are you sure*
> *That we are awake? It seems to me*
> *That yet we sleep, we dream.*
>
> (IV.1.184–91)

The image of mountains which at a distance seem like clouds – things huge and solid turned into mere vapours – aptly suggests the elusive quality of the experience which the lovers are going through at this moment, and is reinforced by the uncertainties of seeing double, finding something which appears to be both one's own and not one's own, and Demetrius' doubt as to whether they are waking or sleeping. The normal confidence of knowing where one is and what one is doing is dissolved at such a moment, producing anxiety and uncertainty; but also, as shown by Bottom's awaking, which comes immediately after this dialogue of the lovers, and his inspiration for a ballad to be called 'Bottom's Dream', such uncertainty can release hitherto unthought of acts of the imagination. If it is an anxious experience, it is also a potentially fruitful one.

Moonlight has a similarly elusive quality. The play abounds in references to it, from the opening with its triple repetition of 'moon' and its contrasting images of the old moon as 'a step-dame or a dowager' and the new moon as 'silver bow/New-bent in heaven'; to Lysander's reference to Phoebe, goddess of the moon, beholding 'her silver visage in the wat'ry glass' (I.1.210); Titania's references to the

moon as 'the governess of floods,/Pale in her anger' (II.1.103–4) and
as weeping with 'a wat'ry eye' (III.1.183); and Oberon's 'Ill met by
moonlight' (II.1.60) and his claim that 'We the globe can compass
soon,/Swifter than the wand'ring moon' (IV.1.94–5). The Athenian
workmen's insistence on the need for a tangible embodiment of
'moonshine' in their play of 'Pyramus and Thisby' is a further reminder
of the importance of the moon in conjunction with a work of the
imagination, while at the same time being indicative of their utter
failure to understand how the imagination operates more by suggestion
than direct representation. Their 'moon', complete with dog, thorn
bush and man-in-the-moon, is, however, a most effective foil to the
changeable, angry, weeping, swiftly flying moon created through the
poetic language of *A Midsummer Night's Dream*. The one is solidly
there on the stage, a prosaic, visible reality, but completely un-
convincing; the other shines nowhere except in the poetry, which
suggests rather than states its existence, but is a pervasive and potent
influence.

Such moonlight is also dream-light, and does, indeed, come very
close to being identified with it in the speech made by Puck when he
prepares the way for the entry of the fairies at the end of the play:

And we fairies, that do run
By the triple Hecate's team
From the presence of the sun,
Following darkness like a dream,
Now are frolic.

(V.1.372–6)

One of Hecate's attributes is that of goddess of the moon, and Puck's
statement that the fairies run by her chariot away from the sun
emphasises her association with powers that are the antithesis of
ordinary sun-lit, i.e. daylight, reality. That in the process they also
follow darkness 'like a dream', that is, belong, as a dream belongs, to
the mysterious world which is the opposite of daylight, makes moon
and dream virtually identical, or at least closely associated ideas.

They certainly come together, as these lines indicate, in the
fairies. When Oberon enters, at the conclusion of this speech by Puck,
his first line is, 'Through the house give *glimmering* light', the word
'glimmering' possibly referring to tapers, but more likely to the fitful,
uncertain light associated with the moon. This is the light both of magic
and the imagination, a supernatural light, not merely in the sense that
it has to do with ghosts (though these are mentioned in Puck's
speech), but in the sense that it is a light by which more than
ordinary, commonplace things are seen and done. It is the sort of

light without which such a play as *A Midsummer Night's Dream* could not exist. Midsummer night is itself a magical time, when, if the proper rites are observed, maids may get glimpses of their future husbands: It is a time when young people roam the woods and wild places that they would normally shun, when their emotions are unusually intense and their imaginations highly wrought. What they see they see by the light of the moon – risking both illumination and deception. When the audience enters the theatre for a performance of *A Midsummer Night's Dream* it also enters on a magical midsummer expedition into the woods and wild places of the imagination, a dream-world where things quite out of the ordinary can happen, and do happen, in abundance. And, as the very first words spoken by Theseus and Hippolyta so strikingly emphasise, the light they are given to see by is the light of the moon.

Part 4

Hints for study

The first thing is to make sure that you are clear in your mind about the relationships between the various characters. Theseus, having conquered Hippolyta in battle, but subsequently won her consent to be his wife, is, at the beginning of the play, eagerly awaiting his wedding day. Their marriage takes place, off-stage, between the end of Act IV, Scene 1 and the beginning of Act V, Scene 1.

Oberon and Titania when we first encounter them (II.1) are in the middle of a quarrel about an Indian boy. Because she will not give up the boy, Oberon takes revenge by making her fall in love with Bottom, transformed by means of the ass's head. She surrenders the boy, and in Act IV, Scene 1 is restored to her normal senses.

The relationships between the young lovers are more intricate. To begin with, Hermia loves Lysander, and Lysander loves her, but Egeus intends her to marry Demetrius. Helena loves Demetrius, but is rejected by him in favour of Hermia. In the wood Oberon tells Puck to make Demetrius fall in love with Helena, but by mistake it is Lysander who is caused to fall in love with her. Demetrius is later made to change his love from Hermia to Helena, so that the situation becomes: Helena loved by both Lysander and Demetrius; Hermia rejected by Lysander. After quarrels among the lovers, Lysander is made to fall in love with Hermia again, and so a happy solution is arrived at, with mutual love between Hermia and Lysander, as at the beginning of the play, and Helena loving Demetrius and being loved by him in return. Confusion about these relationships can be avoided if it is remembered that the *ideal* pairing is Hermia – Lysander and Helena – Demetrius, but that the men change from both loving Hermia, to both loving Helena, before they finally reach the ideal pairing.

While the Athenian workmen are rehearsing their play Puck comes upon them and puts an ass's head on Bottom's shoulders. In this form Bottom finds himself beloved of Titania. When she is restored to her senses, he also is restored to his normal shape and rejoins the workmen. The performance of 'Pyramus and Thisby' takes place before the audience of Theseus, Hippolyta and the lovers. (Remember also that in the play-within-the-play Pyramus and Thisby love each other, but that their love is opposed by their parents. They therefore plan a secret meeting. Thisby arrives first, is scared by a lion, and runs away, dropping her blood-stained mantle. Later Pyramus arrives, finds the mantle, thinks Thisby is dead, and kills himself. Thisby returning finds Pyramus' dead body, and herself commits suicide.)

On this basic plot material it is now necessary to build a more complex understanding of the relationships. Because Shakespeare includes four groups of characters in *A Midsummer Night's Dream* rather than only one or two, the variety of dramatic possibilities is thereby greatly increased, and he exploits this variety to the full. Try to work out the use which he makes of these possibilities. Note how the characters contrast or interact with one another; who appears on stage with whom, when and why; and consider the way in which these encounters, and what the characters say to each other, or in soliloquy (or what is said about them by some commentator such as Puck) either contribute to the play's comic effect, or develop such major themes as 'love' and 'reason'. (For greater detail of this kind see sample answer 3, pp.81–3.)

Because it is an Elizabethan, and not a modern, comedy you should be aware that *A Midsummer Night's Dream* needs to be judged in its own historical context. Something has been said in the foregoing pages about its debt to the extravagantly idealised love which figures in romantic literature and which was carried over into the love poetry of Elizabethan times. To appreciate the style and attitudes which were typical of this poetry it would be useful to read one or two of the sonnets of the period, e.g. Sidney's *Astrophel and Stella,* No. 42, 'O eyes which do the spheres of beauty move', and No. 100, 'O tears! no tears, but rain from Beauty's skies' (to be found in the Everyman *Silver Poets of the Sixteenth Century*, pp.188 and 210) and Spenser's *Amoretti* No. 3, 'The sovereign beauty which I do admire', and No. 81, 'Fair is my love, when her golden hairs' (Everyman *The Shepherd's Calendar and Other Poems,* pp.282 and 311). As an example of the way in which Shakespeare reacted against this excessive idealisation of feminine beauty, read his Sonnet No. 130, 'My mistress' eyes are nothing like the sun' (the Alexander edition of the *Complete Works,* p.1330). Shakespeare rejects all the stock comparisons – his mistress does *not* have eyes like the sun, her lips are *not* as red as coral, her breasts are *not* as white as snow, etc. Indeed, her breath smells ('reeks' is the much stronger word that Shakespeare actually uses), and she does not walk like a goddess, but 'treads on the ground'. 'And yet,' he concludes,

> *by heaven, I think my love as rare*
> *As any she belied with false compare.*

This will help you to appreciate the comic effect when Demetrius addresses Helena in such terms as 'O Helen, goddess, nymph, perfect, divine!' (III.2.137 etc.).

The importance attached in Elizabethan times to order and obedience helps to explain the emphasis on parental authority at the beginning of the play, and can be better understood by reading Ulysses' speech on 'degree' (order, rank in society) in *Troilus and Cressida*, (I.3.75–137) and E.M.W. Tillyard's study of the intellectual background of Shakespeare's day, *The Elizabethan World Picture*. Material about the English countryside and country superstitions, from which much of the poetry and some of the fairy lore of *A Midsummer Night's Dream* is drawn, is usefully presented, through extracts from contemporary Elizabethan writers, in J. Dover Wilson's *Life in Shakespeare's England*; but outside help is less necessary here as so much of the relevant material is included in the text of the play itself, notably in the speeches by the Fairy and Puck in II.1.32–57 and by Titania in II.1.81–117.

Some understanding of the structure and conventions of the Elizabethan theatre is essential. These are discussed in the Introduction (pp.11–14), where some indication is also given of the way in which they influence Shakespeare's plays and condition audience response. When reading *A Midsummer Night's Dream* you should always try to envisage how it would look and sound on the Elizabethan stage. Especially bear in mind that the act and scene divisions, which are useful for identifying particular passages when analysing the text, have little or no relevance to Elizabethan stage production. One 'scene' flowed almost imperceptibly into the next, making for a highly fluid and rapid performance of the play.

In the study of a poetic play like *A Midsummer Night's Dream* the language must also receive careful attention. The historical element is important here, too, since many words used by Shakespeare and his contemporaries no longer form part of current English (e.g. 'an' = if; 'fell' = fierce; 'reremice' = bats; 'minimus' = diminutive creature; and 'welkin' = sky). What is more misleading for the unwary student is the fact that some words are still in use, but with a different meaning (e.g. 'pensioners', in 'The cowslips tall her pensioners be', II.1.10, = followers, or bodyguard, not as in modern 'old age pensioners'; 'weed' in 'Weed wide enough to wrap a fairy in', II.1.256, = garment; and 'Egypt', in 'Sees Helen's beauty in a brow of Egypt', V.1.11, = gypsy). Some, but not all, of these meanings are pointed out in Part II. The wary student will have a well annotated text to hand, and keep referring to the notes. The Glossary in Alexander's text is useful.

Above all, however, it is the imaginative variety and expressiveness of Shakespeare's language which most needs attention. Much of the commentary in Parts II and III has, in fact, been taken up with analysis of language and poetic effect. This should be studied carefully, and the student should try to extend the discussion of nature references, verse forms and patterning of language by finding additional examples of his own. A valuable exercise is to select a speech or passage of dialogue which comes at a particularly interesting moment in the play, and try to understand in detail how the language contributes to the dramatic effect, or heightens the atmosphere which you think Shakespeare is trying to create at that point. Begin by settling the context of the passage and making clear exactly what is happening at this point in the play, and then go on to comment on the way in which language is used to heighten the dramatic effect. Add any further comments on style and versification which seem called for, and try to relate the details which you have observed in the given passage to the overall purpose of the play. (An example of the recommended approach is given in sample answer 1, below.)

In answering more general questions on the themes and characters of *A Midsummer Night's Dream* it is equally important to make exact and careful reference to the text of the play and to support your remarks by illuminating quotations. On the other hand, avoid tedious excess of detail and the bad habit of quoting merely for quotation's sake. Put down only *relevant* material. To ensure this, always think before writing (it is often useful to jot down one or two rough notes first, and then arrange them in a plan); and when you do begin writing come to your main points quickly without a lengthy introduction.

With questions that call for comparison and contrast be especially sure that your answer has a clear and well-designed structure so that no confusion arises over the points of similarity and dissimilarity. (See sample answer 2, pp.79–81.) Conclude briefly, but emphatically, so that your answer does not seem to hang limply in mid-air.

Sample questions and answers

(1) Comment on the dramatic effectiveness and appropriateness of the language in the following passage:

LYS. *Stay, gentle Helena; hear my excuse;*
      My love, my life, my soul, fair Helena!
HEL. *O excellent!*
HER. *Sweet, do not scorn her so.*
DEM. *If she cannot entreat, I can compel.*
LYS. *Thou canst compel no more than she entreat;*
      Thy threats have no more strength than her weak prayers.
      Helen, I love thee, by my life I do;

> *I swear by that which I will lose for thee*
> *To prove him false that says I love thee not.*
> DEM. *I say I love thee more than he can do.*
> LYS. *If thou say so, withdraw, and prove it too.*
> DEM. *Quick, come.*
> HER. *Lysander, whereto tends all this?*
> LYS. *Away, you Ethiope!*
> DEM. *No, no, he will*
> *Seem to break loose – take on as you would follow,*
> *But yet come not. You are a tame man; go!*
> LYS. *Hang off, thou cat, thou burr; vile thing, let loose,*
> *Or I will shake thee from me like a serpent.*

> (III.2.245–61)

This particular passage comes from III.2, the scene in which Demetrius is made to fall in love with Helena (Lysander having already changed his love from Hermia to Helena in II.2). Hermia is still puzzled about what has happened, but Helena believes that Hermia is in league with the men to make fun of her. She makes as if to leave them, and Lysander tries to detain her with the opening words of this passage: 'Stay, gentle Helena . . .' Helena's 'O excellent!' is an ironic retort. She thinks that a trick is being played on her, and so she mockingly applauds it as 'excellent'. In effect she is saying, 'How clever of you all to join together in making fun of such a poor, defenceless creature as I am!' Hermia, still thinking that she has some influence over Lysander, begs him not to continue making fun of Helena. Demetrius, assuming the right of a lover of Helena, says that if Hermia cannot persuade Lysander to stop making fun of Helena he (Demetrius) will *force* Lysander to do so. Lysander retorts that Demetrius' force means no more to him than Hermia's entreaties, and turns to Helena to continue swearing his love for her. This quickly leads to a quarrel between Lysander and Demetrius and a challenge to a duel. Hermia tries to hold Lysander back, and gets abused for her pains, while Demetrius claims that Lysander is not really being detained against his will, but is using Hermia's hold as a cover for his 'tameness', i.e. cowardice.

Lysander's declaration of love for Helena (at lines 246 and 251–3) is sincere, in the sense that he thinks he means what he says, but the words he uses are so much the hackneyed and conventional phraseology of romantic love that the value of that 'love' is called into question. We, the audience, know, of course, that he is under the influence of the love-juice, which accounts for his seemingly automaton-like behaviour; but the language and the situation together inevitably make mockery of the romantic idea that love is aroused by the perfection of the beloved. Lysander seems completely oblivious, when he calls Helena his 'love', his 'life' and his 'soul', that he had previously used much the same language to Hermia, and that the woman he now insults with 'thou cat, thou burr' and 'vile thing' had previously been his 'beauteous' (I.1.104), 'gentle' (I.1.161), 'fair' (II.1.35), 'sweet' (II.1.45) Hermia. We are reminded of the truth of Helena's remarks towards the end of I.1 that because of his lack of judgement Cupid is said to be a child and represented as blind. What passes for 'love' in romantic parlance is very often, in fact, no more than subjective illusion – though, as we see even in such a brief extract as this, an illusion which can have drastic effects on people's behaviour.

In trying to free himself from Hermia's embrace it is interesting to note that Lysander declares, 'let loose,/Or I will shake thee from me like a serpent' (lines 260–1) – words which recall Hermia's dream from which she wakes with a start, exclaiming,

> *Help me, Lysander, help me; do thy best*
> *To pluck this crawling serpent from my breast.*
>
> (II.2.145–6)

She dreamt, she says, that this serpent was eating her heart away while Lysander 'sat smiling' at its 'cruel prey' (line 150). On waking she finds that Lysander has left her, but it is only now, in III.2, that she begins to realise that Lysander has not merely left, but deserted and betrayed her. The reminder of her dream which is given us in Lysander's phrase, 'like a serpent', thus greatly intensifies the emotional pressure of the scene. It also, incidentally, reminds us that a 'dream' can come true, and in a play which is itself 'a midsummer night's *dream*' this has a curious effect. It makes us think of the special sort of 'truth' which can be communicated by seemingly unreal dreams or the imaginative creations of the poet.

Only a limited use of rhyme is made in this particular passage (line 254 rhymes with 255 and 258 with 259), but enough to establish the rather neat, artificial quality of the language, and so prevent us from taking it too seriously. Similarly, the verbal patterning of lines 248–9 has a slightly self-conscious air about it. Demetrius' 'If *she* cannot *entreat, I* can *compel*' is rearranged in reverse order in Lysander's reply, '*Thou* canst *compel* no more than *she entreat*'. Lysander's 'Thou' corresponds to Demetrius' 'I', and so what happens is that the second half of line 248 becomes the first half of line 249, while the first half of line 248 (with slight alteration of the negative form) becomes the second half of line 249 – like changing partners in a dance. The formal patterning of all this tacitly reminds us that, despite the anger and heartaches being generated, the scene we are now witnessing is part of a contrived situation in a comedy which is destined for a happy ending. As Puck later says,

> *Jack shall have Jill;*
> *Nought shall go ill;*
> *The man shall have his mare again, and all shall be well.*
>
> (III.2.461–3)

(The following are some other passages which you might try to analyse for yourself:

(a) Theseus' speech beginning, 'Therefore, fair Hermia, question your desires', I.1.65–78. Note, in particular, the association of 'youth' with 'blood' and the images which associate virginity with isolation and barrenness, including 'the cold fruitless moon'.

(b) Puck's interruption of the workmen's rehearsal and his putting the ass's head on Bottom, III.1.68–109. In this passage there are interesting differences between the prose of the workmen themselves, which is full of illiterate errors, the verse which they speak when acting their parts in 'Pyramus and Thisby', and the verse spoken by Puck.

(c) Puck's speech beginning, 'Now the hungry lion roars', V.1.360–79. Note especially the great breadth of reference, ranging from wild animals and a snoring ploughman, through screech-owls and ghosts, the Fairies and Hecate, to a mouse and the broom with which Puck is 'to sweep the dust behind the door'.)

---

(2) What in your opinion is the relative importance of Theseus and Oberon in the conduct of *A Midsummer Night's Dream* and its poetic significance?

Theseus and Oberon are the two characters in *A Midsummer Night's Dream* who hold positions of the greatest authority and power. Oberon as King of the Fairies rules over the worlds of nature and the supernatural. He shares some of this power with his consort, Titania, but is nevertheless her superior – her husband, lord and master. He is virtually a law unto himself. Theseus, although best known as a classical hero, appears in this play as 'Duke Theseus', more like an Elizabethan aristocrat than a Greek warrior. It is his business to govern Athens and preside over public affairs. Unlike Oberon, he must act within the limits of established order and custom.

Theseus has three roles to perform: he is ruler, social leader, and chief representative of common sense and rationality. As ruler he becomes involved in the Egeus – Hermia dispute, where we see him characteristically upholding law and order. The Athenian law gives a father complete authority over his child, and so when Hermia pleads for the right to choose a husband for herself, saying, 'I would my father look'd but with my eyes', he replies, in similar phrase, but with opposite meaning, 'Rather your eyes must with his judgement look'. He also gives a severe, but not unkindly warning of the consequences to Hermia if she disobeys.

His behaviour here also illustrates his good sense, as does his taking Egeus and Demetrius tactfully aside to have a private word with them. His social role is seen in his hunting and the hearty way he greets the lovers in Act IV, but especially in his function as host at the wedding celebrations in Act V. This last is also the scene in which his rationality and good sense are most clearly expressed, for example, through his speech on 'the lunatic, the lover, and the poet' (especially its emphasis on 'cool reason') and the tolerance which he extends to the workmen's play.

Theseus is thus a significant figure in the play, whose actions and attitudes have considerable influence. Compared with Oberon, however, he is seen to have less control over what actually happens. The Egeus – Hermia problem, which looked such a serious one at the beginning of the play, and which promised to be a difficult one for him to resolve, without either doing damage to justice or hurt to Hermia, simply disappears, as far as he is concerned, when the lovers are found to be paired off amicably. It is Oberon who has, in fact, brought this about. His ability to find and use the magic power of 'Love-in-idleness', though it at first goes wrong through the mistakes of Puck, ensures that the lovers ultimately come together in the right way, and that the comedy reaches its happy ending. Titania's falling in and out of love with the ass-headed Bottom is further testimony to this magical ability of Oberon. His power, in fact, is not merely natural, like Theseus's, but supernatural; and this is demonstrated again at the end of the play when he blesses the marriages of Theseus and Hippolyta and the two pairs of young lovers. All the characters of *A Midsummer Night's Dream* are to this extent dependent on Oberon. Moreover, it is clear that he has powers which are denied even to fellow-supernatural characters. For example, when describing the magic flower, he says to Puck:

> *That very time I saw,* but thou couldst not,
> *Flying between the cold moon and the earth*
> *Cupid, all arm'd.*

The words in roman type put a certain distance between Oberon and even his beloved lieutenant, Puck.

Oberon's ability to see Cupid also suggests that he has some affinity with the gods, a point reinforced when he says, in III.2, 'I with the Morning's love have oft made sport'. On the simplest level this merely means that he is allowed to continue his sport into the morning whereas other supernatural beings are banished at dawn, but it may also mean that he is an accepted companion of Aurora, the goddess of the Dawn – one who is thought fit company for the immortals. His proud, almost haughty bearing further supports this impression that he is an immensely powerful and confident being. He addresses even Titania in a peremptory manner: 'Ill met by moonlight, proud Titania' (though we must remember that he is in a quarrel with her at this point); and, though he is often indulgent to Puck, he rebukes him for his mischievous mistakes quite sharply.

Above all, however, it is the rich, exotic poetry given to Oberon that makes him seem so different from, and, in the end, more impressive than, Theseus. Theseus says nothing to compare in mysterious evocativeness with Oberon's description of the mermaid's singing (II.1.148–54). Such words associate Oberon with a world undreamt of in Theseus' philosophy – a world of incredibly beautiful music (sung by the mythical half-woman, half-fish 'mermaid') which has the power to calm tempestuous seas and send stars shooting through the heavens. This, in fact, is the world of the creative imagination, acknowledged by Theseus in an uncharacteristic moment when he tells how 'imagination bodies forth/The forms of things unknown', but in general discounted by Theseus as idle and deceptive. The reality and force of this imaginative power is made manifest, however, both in the action and the language of the play, and because it is especially embodied in Oberon it is Oberon rather than the admittedly more amiable and humane Theseus who appears the more mysterious, powerful and dominating character.

---

(3) There are four different groups of characters in *A Midsummer Night's Dream*. Show how Shakespeare uses this variety to heighten his dramatic and comic effect.

The four groups are: Theseus and Hippolyta; the young lovers, Lysander, Demetrius, Hermia and Helena; Bottom and the Athenian workmen; Oberon, Titania and the Fairies. There are several ways in which this multiplicity of groups heightens the comic and dramatic effect of the play. The mere fact of variety in itself is a source of interest and entertainment. New faces are constantly appearing and new voices are heard. The coarse, home-spun language and humour of the Athenian workmen gives way to the stylised, romantic language of the lovers; the sound common sense of Theseus alternates with the delicate filigree world of Titania and the Fairies, or the boisterous irresponsibility of Puck's practical jokes. Both visually and aurally it is a play which is constantly changing. No audience need be bored.

This variety also offers a rich field for contrast. The most obvious example is the spectacle of the delicate Titania, Queen of the Fairies, falling in love with the gross Bottom – made even grosser than usual by the ass's head. The play is full of such burlesque absurdities.

Contrast also comes from the rapid switching from one situation to another. For example, at the end of II.2. Hermia, whom we know to have been deserted by Lysander, wakes from a dream of being attacked by a serpent to find that her lover is no longer near her. She goes off in great distress, saying, 'Either death or you I'll find immediately'. This is followed straight away in III.1 by the rehearsal of the play-within-the-play with its very different, farcical atmosphere. Within a few lines Bottom is expressing anxiety that 'this *comedy* of Pyramus and Thisby' will not please because Pyramus 'must draw a sword to kill himself'. Thus, the tension created by Hermia's serious anxiety and reference to death dissolves into the laughter caused by Bottom's spurious anxiety over Pyramus' death.

Further contrast is provided by the fact that Titania, who had fallen asleep near the beginning of II.2, is still sleeping at the back of the stage through both Hermia's and the workmen's scenes, thus keeping the audience aware, while all these other actions are going on, of her (Titania's) character and situation, which are different again from those of both Hermia and the workmen.

However, not only contrasts, but also comparisons are suggested by the variety of characters in this play. The Fairies, for example, who are presented as very different beings from the young lovers, nevertheless prove to be very similar to them in the pettiness of their squabbling and quarrelling; and Theseus and Hippolyta, though in love during the time of the play, are also known to have fought each other in the past. (And who knows what the future may hold for their marriage?) Thus, each character, whatever his or her nature may be, is seen to have an essentially human touch of fallibility.

Again, Bottom is uneducated and has ridiculously naive ideas about dramatic performances, but we see that he makes a sounder comment on reason and love ('reason and love keep little company together now-a-days', III.1.132–3) than Lysander when he changes from Hermia to Helena ('The will of man is by his reason sway'd', II.2.115). And, surprising though it may seem, Bottom's attitude has something in common with that of Theseus when he says that the lover 'sees Helen's beauty in a brow of Egypt' (V.1.11), and even of Helena, at least when she says, 'Nor hath Love's mind of any judgment taste' (I.1.236). These comparisons make us realise that Bottom is not as stupid as he may at first appear; and that those who are better educated are not necessarily *wiser* than he.

Most important of all, the range of character and situation in *A Midsummer Night's Dream* strengthens its claim to be considered as a broadly representative Elizabethan comedy. It does not focus exclusively on a quartet of romantic lovers, but connects them up and down the social scale – upwards to Theseus, the 'Duke' of Athens, and downwards to Bottom and the Athenian workmen. Furthermore, it goes beyond even the human social scale, connecting the lovers, and the other mortals, with the supernatural world of the Fairies. And, as we have seen, this connected variety of human and supernatural characters prompts reflections on wisdom which transcend conventional ideas about social status. In this respect Theseus' acceptance of whatever his subjects can offer, regardless of their social position and ability – valuing their good will above the actual standard of their performance ('what poor duty cannot do, noble respect/Takes it in might, not merit', V.1.91–2) – indicates an enlightened attitude and a type of response which the play would seem to demand of its audience. Above all, it signifies a harmonious relationship in the society which is here being so comprehensively represented. All are included in a fundamentally benign order. It is singularly appropriate, therefore, that all the characters come together in the last act, in the celebration of a wedding, symbol of reconciliation, fertility and hope for the future. Variety has to pass through some discord, but it ends triumphantly in unity.

Practice questions

The following questions are based on material covered in various places in these Notes. Students may find it useful to think about them, and should practise writing answers to them, following the lines suggested above.

1. Suggest how any one scene of *A Midsummer Night's Dream* might have been produced on the Elizabethan stage.
2. What differences would you expect to find if you could see a modern production of *A Midsummer Night's Dream* and then be transported back in time to an Elizabethan production?
3. In what ways are the fairies unlike the human characters, and in what ways are they similar?
4. Do you think that Theseus' speech at the beginning of Act V expresses ideas which are supported by the play as a whole?
5. Is love treated as merely laughable folly in *A Midsummer Night's Dream*?

6. What are Puck's functions? How far do you find yourself liking and approving of him?
7. Is Bottom a character to be laughed *at* or laughed *with*?
8. Discuss the use of contrast, both of character and atmosphere, in *A Midsummer Night's Dream*.
9. 'The play has tragic possibilities at certain moments, but we always have the feeling that things will work out happily in the end.' Would you agree with this statement? If so, suggest some of the ways in which Shakespeare manages to keep this feeling alive in us.
10. Discuss the significance of *one* of the following in *A Midsummer Night's Dream*: dreaming; the moon; illusion; reason; nature.
11. Illustrate the variety of verse-forms used in *A Midsummer Night's Dream*. What dramatic use does Shakespeare make of this variety?
12. What links are there between the play-within-the-play of 'Pyramus and Thisby' and the larger play which is *A Midsummer Night's Dream* itself?

Part 5

Suggestions for further reading

The text

The text used throughout these Notes, and recommended to students particularly because it includes the rest of Shakespeare's plays and poems, is *William Shakespeare, The Complete Works,* edited by Peter Alexander, Collins, London, 1951 – and frequently reprinted. The best annotated text for the non-specialist reader is *A Midsummer Night's Dream,* edited by Stanley Wells (New Penguin Shakespeare), Penguin Books, Harmondsworth, 1967 – and frequently reprinted. Wells' Introduction is also thoroughly recommended, especially for its emphasis on *A Midsummer Night's Dream* as a stage play.

Critical, biographical and background studies

ADAMS, J.C.: *The Globe Playhouse, Its Design and Equipment,* Harvard University Press, Harvard, 1943. Useful for reference on details of Shakespeare's Globe Theatre.

BROWN, J.R.: *Shakespeare and his Comedies,* Methuen, London, 1957. Chapter IV deals with *A Midsummer Night's Dream,* emphasising the special sort of 'truth' with which this play is concerned.

BULLOUGH, G. (ED.): *Narrative and Dramatic Sources of Shakespeare,* Volume 1, Routledge and Kegan Paul, London, 1957. This volume includes a discussion of possible sources for *A Midsummer Night's Dream* and reprints relevant extracts from them.

CHAMBERS, E.K.: *A Short Life of Shakespeare,* Oxford University Press, Oxford, 1933. A useful abridgement by Charles Williams of the two-volume *William Shakespeare: A Study of Facts and Problems* by E.K. Chambers. Gives information on Shakespeare's life and the company of actors with which he was associated, and reprints contemporary records and allusions.

HALLIDAY, F.E.: *Shakespeare in His Age,* Gerald Duckworth, London, 1956. Sketches the historical and cultural (including theatrical) background to Shakespeare's life and work.

FENDER, STEPHEN: *Shakespeare: A Midsummer Night's Dream,* Edward Arnold, London, 1968. A detailed study of the language and themes of the play, written at a level appropriate to English sixth-form 'A' level candidates and first-year university students.

YOUNG, DAVID P.: *Something of Great Constancy, The Art of 'A Midsummer Night's Dream,* Yale University Press, Yale, New Haven, 1966. The best and fullest study of this play. Covers every aspect, and is particularly good on the literary and popular contexts from which *A Midsummer Night's Dream* arises, and on its treatment of illusion.

WILSON, JOHN DOVER (ED.): *Life in Shakespeare's England,* Cambridge University Press, Cambridge, 1911, reprinted Penguin Books, London, 1944. An anthology of Elizabethan writings chosen to illustrate life in Shakespeare's age. Sections II and III on 'The Countryside' and 'Superstition' particularly useful in connection with *A Midsummer Night's Dream.*

The author of these notes

R.P. DRAPER who is Professor of English at the University of Aberdeen was educated at the University of Nottingham. He has held lectureships at the University of Adelaide, South Australia and at the University of Leicester. His publications include: *D.H. Lawrence* (1964); *D.H. Lawrence* (Profiles Series, 1969); and *D.H. Lawrence: The Critical Heritage* (1970). He has also edited Hardy, *The Tragic Novels* (1975) and George Eliot, *The Mill on the Floss* and *Silas Marner* (1977); his book *Tragedy* is forthcoming.